sept.

Della

FARMHOUSE
ENTERTAINING
COOKBOOK

TASTE OF HOME BOOKS • RDA ENTHUSIAST BRANDS, LLC • MILWAUKEE, WI

© 2022 RDA Enthusiast Brands, LLC.
1610 N. 2nd St., Suite 102, Milwaukee WI 53212-3906
All rights reserved. Taste of Home is a registered trademark of RDA
Enthusiast Brands, LLC.
Visit us at tasteofhome.com for other Taste of Home books and products.

ISBN: 978-1-62145-832-6

Executive Editor: Mark Hagen
Senior Art Director: Raeann Thompson
Editor: Amy Glander
Designer: Carrie Peterson
Deputy Editor, Copy Desk: Dulcie Shoener
Senior Copy Editor: Ann Walter

Cover
Photographer: Mark Derse
Set Stylist: Stacey Genaw
Food Stylist: Josh Rink

Pictured on front cover:
Mustard & Cranberry Glazed Ham, p. 55; Tuscan-Style Roasted Asparagus,
p. 67; Passover Popovers, p. 56; Lemony Pineapple Iced Tea, p. 125; Moist
Lemon Chiffon Cake, p. 26
Pictured on title page:
Golden Peach Pie, p.114
Pictured on back cover:
Pumpkin Herb Rolls, p. 201; Bring the Outdoors Inside Napkin Ring,
p. 311; Red, White & Blue Dessert, p. 137; Garden Beauty Centerpieces,
p.79; Brined Grilled Turkey Breast, p. 215; Backyard Dominoes, p. 109;
Chocolate Swirl Delight, p. 322

INSTANT POT is a trademark of Double Insight Inc. This publication has not
been authorized, sponsored or otherwise approved by Double Insight Inc.

Printed in China
1 3 5 7 9 10 8 6 4 2

TIME FOR A FINGER-LICKIN', BOOT-SCOOTIN' PARTY!

From sunny picnics and fun-loving barbecues to cute Turkey Day kids' tables and heartwarming Christmas menus, country-inspired celebrations offer the down-home charm everyone loves.

Now you can serve up homespun hospitality no matter what holiday, occasion or season. Simply turn to the 171 finger-licking recipes inside **Farmhouse Entertaining Cookbook**, and you're guaranteed memory-making success.

Shared by real farm-kitchen cooks, these dishes turn any gathering into a good ol' time! Simply look inside for all the stick-to-your-ribs entrees and garden-fresh sides guests crave most. You'll also find icy Mason-jar beverages and blue-ribbon desserts sure to steal the show.

In addition, tips and how-to photos explain the best way to slice ham, make caramel apples and serve cold-brew coffee like a pro. You'll find these hints and dozens of others inside this colorful keepsake cookbook.

Today's hosts agree that a little farmhouse flair goes a long way—whether you're planning an Independence Day bash, a cozy bonfire, a Halloween party or a casual cookie exchange. That's why we also included quick ideas that put your gatherings over the top. Create a few outdoor games, set up a s'mores station, send guests home with autumnal flower arrangements and package sweets in cute containers. It's a cinch! Simply let us show you how.

You'll also find instant ways to bring a touch of the country to your table and home. From creating quaint no-fuss centerpieces and place settings to hanging seasonal wreaths and holiday garland, adding rustic appeal to any room is a snap.

Whether you're hosting an Easter brunch or a Christmas open house, a backyard bash or a comforting Sunday dinner, the recipes, ideas and decorations in **Farmhouse Entertaining Cookbook** make it a delight to serve up a side of country living all year long.

CONTENTS

SPRING FLINGS

AUTUMN GET-TOGETHERS

SUMMER PARTIES

WINTER GATHERINGS

SPRING FLINGS

Step-into-Spring Mixer

Prosciutto-Wrapped Asparagus
with Raspberry Sauce

Meatballs with Chimichurri Sauce

Marinated Olives

Smoked Salmon Bites
with Shallot Sauce

Crisp Caraway Twists

Ham Balls with Mustard Sauce

Spicy Beef Satay

Goat Cheese Spread in
Roasted Pepper Cups

PROSCIUTTO-WRAPPED ASPARAGUS WITH RASPBERRY SAUCE

Grilling the prosciutto with the asparagus gives this appetizer a salty crunch that's perfect for dipping into a sweet glaze. When a delicious appetizer is this easy to prepare, you owe it to yourself to try it!

—*Noelle Myers, Grand Forks, ND*

TAKES: 30 MIN. • **MAKES:** 16 APPETIZERS

⅓ lb. thinly sliced prosciutto or deli ham

16 fresh asparagus spears, trimmed

½ cup seedless raspberry jam

2 Tbsp. balsamic vinegar

1. Cut prosciutto slices in half. Wrap a prosciutto piece around each asparagus spear; secure ends with toothpicks.

2. Grill asparagus, covered, on an oiled rack over medium heat for 6-8 minutes or until prosciutto is crisp, turning once. Discard the toothpicks.

3. In a small microwave-safe bowl, microwave the jam and vinegar on high for 15-20 seconds or until jam is melted. Serve with asparagus.

1 ASPARAGUS SPEAR WITH 1½ TSP. SAUCE: 50 cal., 1g fat (0 sat. fat), 8mg chol., 184mg sod., 7g carb. (7g sugars, 0 fiber), 3g pro. **DIABETIC EXCHANGES:** ½ starch.

MEATBALLS WITH CHIMICHURRI SAUCE

This South American condiment, featuring fresh cilantro and parsley, is more than just a sauce for tossing with meatballs. You'll want plenty for extra dipping.

—*Amy Chase, Vanderhoof, BC*

TAKES: 30 MIN. • **MAKES:** ABOUT 20 (⅔ CUP SAUCE)

1 pkg. (22 oz.) frozen fully cooked Angus beef meatballs
3 garlic cloves, peeled
1 cup packed Italian flat leaf parsley
¼ cup packed fresh cilantro leaves
1 tsp. salt
¼ tsp. coarsely ground black pepper
2 Tbsp. red wine vinegar
½ cup extra virgin olive oil

1. Prepare meatballs according to package directions.

2. Meanwhile, place garlic in a small food processor; pulse until chopped. Add the parsley, cilantro, salt and pepper; pulse until finely chopped. Add vinegar. While processing, gradually add oil in a steady stream.

3. In a large bowl, toss meatballs with a little more than half of the chimichurri sauce. Transfer to a platter. Serve with remaining sauce for dipping.

1 MEATBALL WITH ABOUT 2 TSP. SAUCE: 130 cal., 12g fat (4g sat. fat), 17mg chol., 318mg sod., 2g carb. (0 sugars, 0 fiber), 4g pro.

WINE PAIRINGS

With the varied and intense flavors in incredible appetizers, why not go with some surprising wine choices? Here are some amazing party-friendly options.

For a sparkling wine, try a Spanish **cava**. Made with red or white grapes, cava is a dry, light and minerally alternative to much more expensive champagnes.

A Greek **assyrtiko** is a natural match for shellfish, spinach and feta, but it's versatile enough to serve with other flavors as well. This dry white is fairly new to the import market and can be hard to find—but it's worth seeking out!

For a sweeter option, an Italian **moscato d'Asti** works well with the meat-based appetizers in this chapter. This is a semi sparkling wine, so you get a pleasant zing rather than full-on fizz. Italians call this style of wine frizzante.

If you're looking beyond whites, a **lambrusco frizzante** is a good match for anything with balsamic vinegar or the classic tomato-herb-cheese trifecta. Lambruscos range from sweet to dry, so ask your wine seller for specific recommendations.

As an alternative to wine, a sparkling white grape juice would provide the same light, refreshing zing without the alcohol.

MARINATED OLIVES

These olives are nice to have for get-togethers because they're
simple to make and they'll add a little zest to the buffet table offerings.
—*Marguerite Shaeffer, Sewell, NJ*

PREP: 10 MIN. + MARINATING • **MAKES:** 4 CUPS

2 cups large pimiento-
 stuffed olives, drained
1 cup pitted kalamata
 olives, drained
1 cup pitted medium
 ripe olives, drained
¼ cup olive oil
2 Tbsp. lemon juice
1 Tbsp. minced fresh thyme
 or 1 tsp. dried thyme
2 tsp. minced fresh
 rosemary or ½ tsp. dried
 rosemary, crushed
2 tsp. grated lemon zest
4 garlic cloves, slivered
 Pepper to taste

1. Place olives in a bowl. Combine the remaining ingredients;
pour over olives and stir. Cover and refrigerate for 1-2 days
before serving, stirring several times each day.

2. Olives may be refrigerated for 2 weeks. Serve olives with a
slotted spoon.

¼ **CUP:** 98 cal., 10g fat (1g sat. fat), 0 chol., 572mg sod., 3g carb.
(0 sugars, 0 fiber), 0 pro.

SMOKED SALMON BITES WITH SHALLOT SAUCE

Tangy Dijon-mayo sauce adds zip to layers of crisp arugula, smoked salmon and shaved Asiago cheese. I make these a couple of times a year.
—*Jamie Brown-Miller, Napa, CA*

TAKES: 30 MIN. • MAKES: 25 APPETIZERS

1 sheet frozen puff
   pastry, thawed

SAUCE
2 shallots
2 Tbsp. Dijon mustard
1 Tbsp. mayonnaise
1 Tbsp. red wine vinegar
¼ cup olive oil

FINISHING
1 cup fresh arugula
   or baby spinach,
   coarsely chopped
4½ oz. smoked salmon
   or lox, thinly sliced
½ cup shaved Asiago
   cheese

1. Preheat oven to 400°. Unfold puff pastry; cut into 25 squares. Transfer to greased baking sheets. Bake 11-13 minutes or until golden brown.

2. Meanwhile, grate 1 shallot and finely chop the other. In a small bowl, combine the shallots, mustard, mayonnaise and vinegar. While whisking, gradually add oil in a steady stream. Spoon a small amount of sauce onto each pastry; layer with arugula and salmon. Drizzle with remaining sauce and sprinkle with cheese.

1 APPETIZER: 89 cal., 6g fat (1g sat. fat), 3mg chol., 105mg sod., 6g carb. (0 sugars, 1g fiber), 2g pro.

CRISP CARAWAY TWISTS

This appetizer is always a hit when I serve it on holidays or special occasions. The flaky cheese-filled twists (made with convenient puff pastry) bake to a crispy golden brown. When our big family gets together, I make two batches.

—Dorothy Smith, El Dorado, AR

TAKES: 30 MIN. • MAKES: ABOUT 1½ DOZEN

1 large egg
1 Tbsp. water
1 tsp. country-style Dijon mustard
¾ cup shredded Swiss cheese
¼ cup finely chopped onion
2 tsp. minced fresh parsley
1½ tsp. caraway seeds
¼ tsp. garlic salt
1 sheet frozen puff pastry, thawed

SERVE IT WITH: Pumpkin Black Bean Soup, Page 177

1. In a small bowl, beat egg, water and mustard; set aside. In another bowl, combine the cheese, onion, parsley, caraway seeds and garlic salt.

2. Unfold pastry sheet; brush with egg mixture. Sprinkle cheese mixture lengthwise over half the pastry. Fold pastry over filling; press edges to seal. Brush top with remaining egg mixture. Cut widthwise into ½-in. strips; twist each strip several times.

3. Place 1 in. apart on greased baking sheets, pressing ends down. Bake at 375° for 15-20 minutes or until golden brown. Serve warm.

1 TWIST: 90 cal., 5g fat (2g sat. fat), 15mg chol., 91mg sod., 8g carb. (0 sugars, 1g fiber), 3g pro.

HAM BALLS WITH MUSTARD SAUCE

Any leftover ham is set aside for these crispy little croquettes. I shape them early in the day, then simply fry them at dinnertime. The mustard sauce is mild and pairs well with ham.

—*Kathy Vincek, Toms River, NJ*

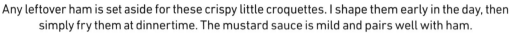

PREP: 35 MIN. + CHILLING • COOK: 5 MIN./BATCH • MAKES: 1 DOZEN

2 cups finely chopped
   fully cooked ham
1 Tbsp. finely
   chopped onion
1 tsp. minced fresh parsley
¼ cup butter, cubed
¼ cup all-purpose flour
¼ tsp. salt
⅛ tsp. pepper
1 cup 2% milk
1 large egg
2 Tbsp. water
¾ cup dry bread crumbs
   Oil for deep-fat frying

SAUCE
1½ tsp. butter
1½ tsp. all-purpose flour
¼ tsp. salt
   Dash pepper
½ cup 2% milk
4½ tsp. yellow mustard

1. In a small bowl, combine the ham, onion and parsley; set the mixture aside.

2. In a small saucepan, melt butter. Stir in the flour, salt and pepper until smooth; gradually add milk. Bring to a boil; cook and stir for 1 minute or until thickened. Stir into ham mixture.

3. Spread into an 8-in. square baking dish; cover and refrigerate for at least 2 hours.

4. In a shallow bowl, combine egg and water. Place bread crumbs in a separate shallow bowl. Shape ham mixture into 12 balls (mixture will be soft); roll each ball in egg mixture, then in bread crumbs. Cover and refrigerate 2 hours longer.

5. In an electric skillet or deep fryer, heat oil to 375°. Fry balls, a few at a time, for 2-3 minutes or until golden brown, turning once. Drain on paper towels.

6. Meanwhile, for the sauce, in a small saucepan, melt butter. Stir in the flour, salt and pepper until smooth; gradually add milk. Bring to a boil; cook and stir for 2 minutes or until thickened. Stir in mustard. Serve with ham balls.

1 APPETIZER WITH 2 TSP. SAUCE: 188 cal., 14g fat (5g sat. fat), 44mg chol., 503mg sod., 8g carb. (2g sugars, 0 fiber), 7g pro.

SPICY BEEF SATAY

The fragrant spices and full flavors of North African cuisine make these appetizers a tasty party food.
—*Roxanne Chan, Albany, CA*

PREP: 35 MIN. • BROIL: 5 MIN. • MAKES: 2 DOZEN (½ CUP SAUCE)

1 cup white wine vinegar
¾ cup sugar
½ cup water
1 Tbsp. orange marmalade
¼ tsp. grated orange zest
¼ tsp. crushed red
    pepper flakes
½ cup finely chopped
    salted roasted almonds
2 Tbsp. minced fresh mint
1 green onion, finely
    chopped
1 Tbsp. lemon juice
1 garlic clove, minced
¼ tsp. each ground
    cinnamon, cumin
    and coriander
1 lb. lean ground
    beef (90% lean)
    Minced fresh parsley

1. In a small saucepan, combine the first 6 ingredients. Bring to a boil. Reduce heat; simmer, uncovered, for 25 minutes or until reduced to ½ cup.

2. Meanwhile, in a large bowl, combine almonds, mint, onion, lemon juice, garlic and spices. Crumble beef over mixture and mix lightly but thoroughly. Divide into 24 pieces. Shape each piece into a 3x1-in. rectangle; insert a soaked wooden appetizer skewer into each piece.

3. Broil 6 in. from the heat 2-4 minutes on each side or until a thermometer reads 160°. Arrange on a serving platter. Drizzle with sauce mixture and sprinkle with parsley.

1 APPETIZER WITH 1 TSP. SAUCE: 74 cal., 3g fat (1g sat. fat), 12mg chol., 25mg sod., 8g carb. (7g sugars, 0 fiber), 4g pro.

KITCHEN TIP: These hearty appetizers make a light meal served alongside a green salad and some bread. Enjoy the skewers over a bed of cooked white rice.

GOAT CHEESE SPREAD IN ROASTED PEPPER CUPS

I had a similar dish in a restaurant in Seattle, and when I returned home I just had to try making it. This is the result, and it's fantastic! I've taken it to work for parties and my boss once commented, "It's so good, it must be illegal."

—*Jenny Rodriquez, Pasco, WA*

PREP: 25 MIN. • **BAKE:** 40 MIN. • **MAKES:** 8 SERVINGS

4 medium sweet
  red peppers
3 Tbsp. olive oil, divided
1 medium onion,
  finely chopped
4 garlic cloves, minced
1 pkg. (8 oz.) cream
  cheese, softened
8 oz. fresh goat
  cheese, softened
1 cup grated Parmesan
  cheese
2 to 3 medium
  tomatoes, seeded
  and finely chopped
2 Tbsp. minced
  fresh cilantro
1 Tbsp. minced
  fresh parsley
½ tsp. hot pepper sauce
⅛ tsp. salt
⅛ tsp. pepper

HERBED GARLIC TOASTS
½ cup butter, softened
1 Tbsp. minced
  fresh parsley
2 garlic cloves, minced
24 slices French bread
   baguette (¼ in. thick)

1. Remove tops and seeds from peppers; rub peppers with 1 Tbsp. oil. Place in an ungreased 8-in. square baking dish. Bake, uncovered, at 350° for 15-20 minutes. Remove from oven; turn peppers upside down in baking dish to drain.

2. In a small skillet, saute onion in remaining oil until tender. Add garlic; cook 1 minute longer. Transfer to a large bowl. Stir in the cheeses, tomatoes, cilantro, parsley, pepper sauce, salt and pepper. Spoon into pepper cups; return to baking dish.

3. Bake, uncovered, at 350° until heated through, 25-30 minutes.

4. Meanwhile, in a small bowl, combine the butter, parsley and garlic; spread over baguette slices. Place on an ungreased baking sheet. Bake until lightly browned, 10-12 minutes. Serve with cheese spread.

½ CUP SPREAD WITH 3 TOASTS: 445 cal., 35g fat (19g sat. fat), 89mg chol., 583mg sod., 23g carb. (5g sugars, 3g fiber), 12g pro.

KITCHEN TIP: Don't have any peppers on hand? Don't worry! Whip up this savory dip on its own and serve in a bowl alongside the garlic toasts.

Spring Brunch

Apricot Ginger
Mustard-Glazed Ham

Sunny Fruit Medley

Favorite Crab Pasta Salad

Roasted Asparagus with Thyme

Easter Egg Bread

Cheesy Sausage Potatoes

Bird Nests

Moist Lemon Chiffon Cake

APRICOT GINGER MUSTARD-GLAZED HAM

One year I decided to bake my ham with a sweet and spicy gingery glaze. This is how we do special-occasion dining.

—Ally Phillips, Murrells Inlet, SC

PREP: 15 MIN. • **BAKE:** 2 HOURS • **MAKES:** 16 SERVINGS

1   **fully cooked bone-in ham (7 to 9 lbs.)**
½   **cup drained canned apricot halves**
½   **cup stone-ground mustard**
⅓   **cup packed brown sugar**
2   **Tbsp. grated fresh gingerroot**
1   **Tbsp. whole peppercorns**
½   **tsp. sea salt**
½   **tsp. coarsely ground pepper**

1. Preheat oven to 325°. Place ham on a rack in a shallow roasting pan. Using a sharp knife, score surface of ham with ¼-in.-deep cuts in a diamond pattern. Cover and bake until a thermometer reads 130°, 1¾-2¼ hours.

2. Meanwhile, place remaining ingredients in a food processor; process until blended. Remove ham from oven. Increase oven setting to 425°. Spread apricot mixture over ham.

3. Bake the ham, uncovered, until a thermometer reads 140°, 15-20 minutes longer. If desired, increase oven setting to broil; broil until golden brown, 2-4 minutes.

4 OZ. COOKED HAM: 201 cal., 6g fat (2g sat. fat), 87mg chol., 1258mg sod., 8g carb. (7g sugars, 0 fiber), 30g pro.

HOW-TO CARVE PERFECT HAM SLICES

Carving a ham is easy! You're just four steps away from beautiful slices worthy of your best brunch serving platter.

STEP 1
Begin by cutting off the cushion (boneless) portion of the meat.

STEP 2
Holding the cushion portion steady with a meat fork, cut it into even slices from the top down.

STEP 3
Cut the remaining (bone-in) portion of the ham horizontally above the bone.

STEP 4
Carve into even vertical slices. Save the remaining bone-in slab for soup.

MOIST LEMON CHIFFON CAKE

This fluffy cake is a real treat drizzled with the sweet-tart lemon glaze.

—Rebecca Baird, Salt Lake City, UT

PREP: 15 MIN. • **BAKE:** 45 MIN. + COOLING • **MAKES:** 16 SERVINGS

½ cup fat-free
evaporated milk
½ cup reduced-fat
sour cream
¼ cup lemon juice
2 Tbsp. canola oil
2 tsp. vanilla extract
1 tsp. grated lemon zest
1 tsp. lemon extract
2 cups cake flour
1½ cups sugar
1 Tbsp. baking powder
½ tsp. salt
1 cup large egg whites
(about 7), room
temperature
½ tsp. cream of tartar

LEMON GLAZE
1¾ cups confectioners' sugar
3 Tbsp. lemon juice

1. In a large bowl, combine the first 7 ingredients. Sift together the flour, sugar, baking powder and salt; gradually beat into lemon mixture until smooth. In a small bowl, beat egg whites until foamy. Add cream of tartar; beat until stiff peaks form. Gently fold into the lemon mixture.

2. Pour into an ungreased 10-in. tube pan. Bake at 325° for 45-55 minutes or until cake springs back when lightly touched. Immediately invert pan; cool completely. Remove the cake to a serving platter. Combine glaze ingredients; drizzle over cake.

1 PIECE: 230 cal., 3g fat (1g sat. fat), 3mg chol., 189mg sod., 47g carb. (33g sugars, 0 fiber), 4g pro.

SUNNY FRUIT MEDLEY

The orange dressing on this salad complements the fresh
fruit flavors beautifully. It's perfect for a spring or summer brunch.

—Karen Bourne, Magrath, AB

PREP: 20 MIN. + CHILLING • MAKES: 10 SERVINGS

2   cups orange juice
1   cup sugar
2   Tbsp. cornstarch
3   cups cubed
    honeydew melon
3   medium firm
    bananas, sliced
2   cups green grapes
2   cups halved fresh
    strawberries

**SERVE
IT WITH:**
Oven Chicken Fingers,
Page 232

1. In a small saucepan, mix the orange juice, sugar and cornstarch until smooth. Bring to a boil, stirring constantly; cook and stir for 2 minutes or until thickened. Transfer to a small bowl; cool slightly. Refrigerate, covered, for at least 2 hours.

2. Just before serving, combine the fruit in a large serving bowl. Drizzle with orange juice mixture; toss gently to coat.

¾ CUP: 188 cal., 1g fat (0 sat. fat), 0 chol., 7mg sod., 47g carb. (41g sugars, 2g fiber), 1g pro.

APPLE-GINGER GLAZED FRUIT: Omit first 3 ingredients. In a small saucepan, mix 2 cups unsweetened apple juice, ¼ cup honey, 2 Tbsp. finely chopped crystallized ginger and 2 Tbsp. lemon juice. Bring to a boil over medium-high heat. Cook and stir 2 minutes or until mixture is reduced to 1½ cups. Remove from heat. Cool. Mix 4 tsp. chopped fresh mint into fruit and drizzle with cooled glaze.

FAVORITE CRAB PASTA SALAD

Wanda, a friend at work, made this for a party and boy, did it catch on
fast! It's especially wonderful for spring gatherings and summer barbecues.

—*Cheryl Seweryn, Lemont, IL*

TAKES: 20 MIN. • MAKES: 7 SERVINGS

3 cups uncooked
   medium pasta shells
1 lb. creamy coleslaw
½ cup mayonnaise
1 Tbsp. chopped onion
1 tsp. dill weed
   Dash salt
2 cups chopped
   imitation crabmeat

1. Cook the pasta according to package directions. Meanwhile, in a large serving bowl, combine coleslaw, mayonnaise, onion, dill and salt. Stir in crab.

2. Drain pasta and rinse in cold water. Add to coleslaw mixture; toss to coat. Chill until serving.

¾ CUP: 376 cal., 20g fat (3g sat. fat), 17mg chol., 508mg sod., 39g carb. (9g sugars, 2g fiber), 10g pro.

HOP INTO SPRING PLACE SETTINGS

Bring a smile to everyone's faces with these adorable place settings. Cut a bunny shape out of pretty patterned paper. Punch a hole near the bottom. Leaving a 2-inch stem, insert a white carnation into the hole.

ROASTED ASPARAGUS WITH THYME

This good-for-you side dish is so easy to prepare, yet it's elegant and special. What a classic way to welcome spring to your table.

—Sharon Leno, Keansburg, NJ

TAKES: 20 MIN. • MAKES: 12 SERVINGS

3 lbs. fresh asparagus, trimmed
3 Tbsp. olive oil
2 tsp. minced fresh thyme or ¾ tsp. dried thyme
½ tsp. salt
¼ tsp. pepper

1. Place asparagus in a baking pan lined with heavy-duty foil. Drizzle with oil and toss to coat. Sprinkle with the thyme, salt and pepper.

2. Bake the asparagus, uncovered, at 425° for 10-15 minutes or until crisp-tender.

7 ASPARAGUS SPEARS: 55 cal., 4g fat (1g sat. fat), 0 chol., 101mg sod., 4g carb. (0 sugars, 1g fiber), 3g pro. **DIABETIC EXCHANGES:** 1 vegetable, ½ fat.

KITCHEN TIP: You can also prepare the asparagus on the stovetop. Simply cut the spears into pieces and stir-fry in the olive oil over medium heat until crisp-tender.

EASTER EGG BREAD

I've made this Easter treat for 20 years! Colored hard-boiled eggs baked in the dough give this sweet bread such a festive look. Leave them out and it can be enjoyed any time of year. My husband especially likes the bread with baked ham.

—Heather Durante, Wellsburg, WV

PREP: 55 MIN. + RISING • **BAKE:** 25 MIN. + COOLING • **MAKES:** 1 LOAF (16 PIECES)

½ cup sugar
2 pkg. (¼ oz. each) active dry yeast
1 to 2 tsp. ground cardamom
1 tsp. salt
6 to 6½ cups all-purpose flour
1½ cups 2% milk
6 Tbsp. butter, cubed
4 large eggs, room temperature, divided use
3 to 6 hard-boiled large eggs, unpeeled
 Assorted food coloring
 Canola oil
2 Tbsp. water

1. In a large bowl, mix sugar, yeast, cardamom, salt and 2 cups flour. In a small saucepan, heat milk and butter to 120°-130°. Add to dry ingredients; beat on medium speed 2 minutes. Add 3 eggs; beat on high 2 minutes. Stir in enough remaining flour to form a soft dough (dough will be sticky).

2. Turn dough onto a floured surface; knead until smooth and elastic, 6-8 minutes. Place in a greased bowl, turning once to grease the top. Cover and let rise in a warm place until doubled, about 45 minutes.

3. Meanwhile, dye hard-boiled eggs with food coloring following package directions. Let stand until completely dry.

4. Punch down dough. Turn onto a lightly floured surface; divide into thirds. Roll each portion into a 24-in. rope. Place ropes on a greased baking sheet and braid. Bring ends together to form a ring. Pinch ends to seal. Lightly coat dyed eggs with oil; arrange on braid, tucking them carefully between ropes.

5. Cover with a kitchen towel; let rise in a warm place until doubled, about 20 minutes. Preheat oven to 375°.

6. In a bowl, whisk remaining egg and water; gently brush over dough, avoiding eggs. Bake until golden brown, 25-30 minutes. Remove from pan to a wire rack to cool. Refrigerate leftovers.

1 PIECE: 281 cal., 8g fat (4g sat. fat), 107mg chol., 231mg sod., 44g carb. (8g sugars, 1g fiber), 9g pro.

CHEESY SAUSAGE POTATOES

For a satisfying brunch, try these tender potato slices with lots of sausage and cheese. Everyone loves them and afterward the pan is always empty.

—Linda Hill, Marseilles, IL

TAKES: 25 MIN. • MAKES: 10 SERVINGS

3 lbs. potatoes, peeled and cut into ¼-in. slices
1 lb. bulk pork sausage
1 medium onion, chopped
¼ cup butter, melted
2 cups shredded cheddar cheese

1. Place potatoes in a large saucepan and cover with water. Bring to a boil. Reduce the heat; simmer, uncovered, until tender, 8-10 minutes. Meanwhile, crumble sausage into a large skillet; add onion. Cook over medium heat until meat is no longer pink; drain if necessary.

2. Drain potatoes; arrange in an ungreased 13x9-in. baking dish. Drizzle with butter. Add the sausage mixture and stir gently. Sprinkle with cheese.

3. Bake, uncovered, at 350° until cheese is melted, 5-7 minutes.

¾ CUP: 252 cal., 13g fat (8g sat. fat), 37mg chol., 220mg sod., 26g carb. (2g sugars, 3g fiber), 9g pro.

KITCHEN TIP: Get creative with the meat and cheese if you'd like. Try ground beef or even spicy chorizo. Consider substituting Swiss or a Mexican cheese blend for the cheddar.

BIRD NESTS

This is a fun, kid-friendly recipe I pulled together a few years ago. My kids love helping me make these.

—Jessica Boivin, Nekoosa, WI

PREP: 40 MIN. • **MAKES:** 2 DOZEN

2   pkg. (10 to 12 oz. each) white baking chips
1   pkg. (10 oz.) pretzel sticks
24 yellow chicks Peeps candy
1   pkg. (12 oz.) M&M's eggs or other egg-shaped candy

1. In a large metal bowl over simmering water, melt baking chips; stir until smooth. Reserve ½ cup melted chips for decorations; keep warm.

2. Add pretzel sticks to remaining chips; stir to coat evenly. Drop mixture into 24 mounds on waxed paper; shape into bird nests using 2 forks.

3. Dip bottoms of Peeps in reserved chips; place in nests. Attach eggs with remaining chips. Let stand until set.

1 NEST: 276 cal., 11g fat (7g sat. fat), 7mg chol., 215mg sod., 41g carb. (30g sugars, 1g fiber), 4g pro.

Easter Egg Decorating Party

Cupcake Easter Baskets

Creamy Macaroni & Cheese

Creamy Deviled Eggs

Special Stuffed Strawberries

Ranch Snack Mix

Marshmallow Easter Eggs

Chicken Cordon Bleu Stromboli

Easter Sugar Cookies

CUPCAKE EASTER BASKETS

These cute cupcakes have a mild orange flavor. It's fun to dress them up for Easter! As we raised four sons and a daughter, I prepared many school lunches and often added these springtime treats.

—Julie Johnston, Shaunavon, SK

PREP: 20 MIN. • **BAKE:** 20 MIN. + COOLING • **MAKES:** 1½ DOZEN

½ cup butter, softened
1 cup sugar
1 large egg, room temperature
1 tsp. grated orange zest
2 cups cake flour
¾ tsp. baking soda
½ tsp. baking powder
¼ tsp. salt
⅔ cup buttermilk

FROSTING
¾ cup butter, softened
6 oz. cream cheese, softened
1 tsp. vanilla extract
3 cups confectioners' sugar
1 tsp. water
4 drops green food coloring
1½ cups sweetened shredded coconut
  Chocolate licorice twists
  Chocolate egg candy

1. Preheat oven to 350°. In a large bowl, cream butter and sugar until light and fluffy, 5-7 minutes. Beat in the egg and orange zest. Combine the flour, baking soda, baking powder and salt; add to creamed mixture alternately with buttermilk.

2. Fill 18 paper-lined muffin cups two-thirds full. Bake until a toothpick comes out clean, 20-25 minutes. Cool for 10 minutes before removing from pans to wire racks to cool completely.

3. For frosting, in a small bowl, beat butter, cream cheese and vanilla until smooth. Gradually beat in confectioners' sugar; spread over cupcakes. Combine water and food coloring in a large bowl; add coconut. Stir to coat. Sprinkle over cupcakes.

4. Using a metal or wooden skewer, poke 2 holes in the top of each cupcake, 1 hole on each side. Cut licorice into 6-in. strips for handles; insert each end of a licorice piece into a hole. Decorate with candy eggs.

1 CUPCAKE: 351 cal., 18g fat (11g sat. fat), 51mg chol., 273mg sod., 47g carb. (33g sugars, 1g fiber), 3g pro.

KITCHEN TIP: Keep this cupcake recipe handy! Whether you make the baskets or not, you'll want to prepare the tender cakes and incredible frosting time and again.

CREAMY MACARONI & CHEESE

This is the ultimate creamy mac and cheese. It's saucy, thick and very rich, with wonderful cheddar flavor. Once you taste it, you'll be hooked.

—*Cindy Hartley, Chesapeake, VA*

PREP: 20 MIN. • BAKE: 35 MIN. • MAKES: 6 SERVINGS

2 cups uncooked elbow macaroni
½ cup butter, cubed
½ cup all-purpose flour
1½ to 2 cups 2% milk
1 cup sour cream
8 oz. cubed Velveeta
¼ cup grated Parmesan cheese
½ tsp. salt
½ tsp. ground mustard
½ tsp. pepper
2 cups shredded cheddar cheese

1. Cook macaroni according to package directions.

2. Meanwhile, preheat oven to 350°. In a large saucepan, melt butter. Stir in flour until smooth. Gradually add 1½ cups milk. Bring to a boil; cook and stir 2 minutes or until thickened. Reduce heat; stir in sour cream, Velveeta, Parmesan cheese, salt, mustard and pepper until smooth and cheese is melted. Add more milk to reach desired consistency.

3. Drain macaroni; toss with cheddar cheese. Transfer to a greased 3-qt. baking dish. Stir in cream sauce.

4. Bake, uncovered, 35-40 minutes or until golden brown and bubbly.

1 CUP: 653 cal., 46g fat (30g sat. fat), 143mg chol., 1141mg sod., 35g carb. (8g sugars, 1g fiber), 25g pro.

SERVE IT WITH:
Apricot Ginger Mustard–Glazed Ham, Page 25

CREAMY DEVILED EGGS

These deviled eggs are nicely flavored with a tang of mustard and a spark of sweetness from pickle relish. We even served them at my daughter's wedding reception.

—Barbara Towler, Derby, OH

PREP: 1 HOUR + CHILLING • **MAKES:** 6 DOZEN

36 hard-boiled large eggs
1 pkg. (8 oz.) cream cheese, softened
1½ cups mayonnaise
⅓ cup sweet pickle relish
⅓ cup Dijon mustard
¾ tsp. salt
¼ tsp. pepper
Optional: Paprika and fresh parsley

1. Slice eggs in half lengthwise; remove yolks and set yolks and whites aside.

2. In a large bowl, beat cream cheese until smooth. Add the mayonnaise, relish, mustard, salt, pepper and reserved yolks; mix well. Stuff or pipe into egg whites. If desired, garnish with paprika and parsley. Refrigerate until serving.

2 STUFFED EGG HALVES: 172 cal., 15g fat (4g sat. fat), 222mg chol., 254mg sod., 2g carb. (1g sugars, 0 fiber), 7g pro.

EASY IDEAS FOR DECORATING EASTER EGGS

Put your party over the top when you offer guests these colorful options sure to make their Easter eggs stand out.

1. DIY EGG DYE
In a glass cup, mix ½ cup boiling water, 1 tsp. white vinegar and drops of food coloring to reach the desired color.

2. MARBLED EFFECT
Add a few drops of food coloring to a bowl of whipped cream, and swirl using a toothpick. Roll eggs in the rainbow mixture and let sit for 45 minutes to an hour before rinsing in water.

3. ADD A MESSAGE
Dip eggs in your choice of homemade or store-bought egg dyes. Let dry, then write words, draw a picture or simply add a pattern on the egg using an opaque white food-safe marker.

4. STAMP A PATTERN
Use mini rubber stamps, such as the flowers shown above, dipped in food dye poured onto a paper towel or napkin. Make sure you choose tiny stamps so you can see the entire shape.

SPECIAL STUFFED STRAWBERRIES

These sweet bites can be made ahead of time, and they look really colorful on a tray. I sometimes sprinkle the piped filling with finely chopped pistachio nuts.

—Marcia Orlando, Boyertown, PA

TAKES: 20 MIN. • MAKES: 2 DOZEN

24 large fresh strawberries
½ cup spreadable strawberry cream cheese
3 Tbsp. sour cream
Graham cracker crumbs

1. Place the strawberries on a cutting board and cut off tops; remove bottom tips so they sit flat. Using a small paring knife, hull out the center of each berry.

2. In a small bowl, beat cream cheese and sour cream until smooth. Pipe or spoon filling into each berry. Top with crushed graham crackers. Refrigerate until serving.

1 STRAWBERRY: 18 cal., 1g fat (1g sat. fat), 4mg chol., 22mg sod., 1g carb. (1g sugars, 0 fiber), 1g pro.

RANCH SNACK MIX

This is wonderful fast-to-fix munchie. The recipe makes a generous 24 cups and doesn't involve any cooking. It's a cinch to make.

—Linda Murphy, Pulaski, WI

TAKES: 15 MIN. • MAKES: 32 SERVINGS (6 QT.)

1 pkg. (12 oz.) miniature pretzels
16 cups Bugles (about 12 oz.)
1 can (10 oz.) salted cashews
1 pkg. (6 oz.) Goldfish cheddar crackers
1 envelope ranch salad dressing mix
¾ cup canola oil

In 2 large bowls, combine the pretzels, Bugles, cashews and crackers. Sprinkle with dressing mix; toss gently to combine. Drizzle with the oil; toss until well coated. Store snack mix in airtight containers.

¾ CUP: 185 cal., 11g fat (2g sat. fat), 2mg chol., 357mg sod., 19g carb. (1g sugars, 1g fiber), 4g pro.

MARSHMALLOW EASTER EGGS

I've been making this wonderful Easter candy for years.
These eggs are a big hit with everyone who loves marshmallows.
—*Betty Claycomb, Alverton, PA*

PREP: 45 MIN. + STANDING • COOK: 15 MIN. • MAKES: ABOUT 3 DOZEN

25 **cups all-purpose**
    flour (about 8 lbs.)
1   **large egg**
2   **Tbsp. unflavored gelatin**
½   **cup cold water**
2   **cups sugar**
1   **cup light corn**
    syrup, divided
¾   **cup hot water**
2   **tsp. vanilla extract**
1   **lb. dark chocolate**
    candy coating, melted
    Candy coating disks,
    multiple colors

1. Spread 7 cups flour in each of three 13x9-in. pans and 4 cups flour in a 9-in. square pan. Carefully wash the egg in a mild bleach solution (1 tsp. chlorine bleach to 1 qt. warm water); dry. Press washed egg halfway into the flour to form an impression. Repeat 35 times, 2 in. apart; set aside.

2. In a small bowl, sprinkle the gelatin over cold water; set aside. In a large saucepan, combine the sugar, ½ cup corn syrup and hot water. Bring to a boil over medium heat, stirring constantly, until a candy thermometer reads 238° (soft-ball stage). Remove from the heat; stir in remaining corn syrup.

3. Pour into a large bowl. Add reserved gelatin, 1 Tbsp. at a time, beating on high speed until candy is thick and has cooled to lukewarm, about 10 minutes. Beat in vanilla.

4. Spoon lukewarm gelatin mixture into egg depressions; dust with flour. Let stand for 3-4 hours or until set.

5. Brush the excess flour off the marshmallow eggs. Dip each egg in chocolate candy coating. Place flat side down on waxed paper. Let stand until set. Drizzle each colored candy coating over eggs.

NOTE: We recommend that you test your candy thermometer before each use by bringing water to a boil; the thermometer should read 212°. Adjust your recipe temperature up or down based on your test.

1 PIECE: 147 cal., 4g fat (4g sat. fat), 0 chol., 7mg sod., 28g carb. (28g sugars, 0 fiber), 1g pro.

KITCHEN TIP: Silicone egg molds are available and can be used instead of the flour.

CHICKEN CORDON BLEU STROMBOLI

If chicken cordon bleu and stromboli had a baby, this would be it. Serve with jarred Alfredo sauce, homemade Alfredo sauce or classic Mornay sauce on the side if desired.

—*Cyndy Gerken, Naples, FL*

TAKES: 30 MIN. • MAKES: 6 SERVINGS

1 tube (13.8 oz.) refrigerated pizza crust
4 thin slices deli ham
1½ cups shredded cooked chicken
6 slices Swiss cheese
1 Tbsp. butter, melted
Roasted garlic Alfredo sauce, optional

SERVE IT WITH:
Grandma's Classic Potato Salad, Page 191

1. Preheat oven to 400°. Unroll pizza dough onto a baking sheet. Layer with ham, chicken and cheese to within ½ in. of edges. Roll up jelly-roll style, starting with a long side; pinch seam to seal and tuck ends under. Brush with melted butter.

2. Bake until crust is dark golden brown, 18-22 minutes. Let stand 5 minutes before slicing. If desired, serve with Alfredo sauce for dipping.

1 PIECE: 298 cal., 10g fat (4g sat. fat), 53mg chol., 580mg sod., 32g carb. (4g sugars, 1g fiber), 21g pro.

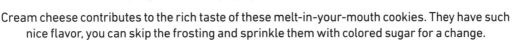

EASTER SUGAR COOKIES

Cream cheese contributes to the rich taste of these melt-in-your-mouth cookies. They have such nice flavor, you can skip the frosting and sprinkle them with colored sugar for a change.

—Julie Brunette, Green Bay, WI

PREP: 15 MIN. + CHILLING • **BAKE:** 10 MIN./BATCH • **MAKES:** 4 DOZEN

1 cup butter, softened
3 oz. cream cheese, softened
1 cup sugar
1 large egg yolk, room temperature
½ tsp. vanilla extract
¼ tsp. almond extract
2¼ cups all-purpose flour
½ tsp. salt
¼ tsp. baking soda
Tinted frosting or colored sugar

1. In a bowl, cream butter, cream cheese and sugar. Beat in egg yolk and extracts. Combine the flour, salt and baking soda; gradually add to creamed mixture. Cover and refrigerate for 3 hours or until easy to handle.

2. Preheat oven to 375°. On a lightly floured surface, roll out dough to ⅛-in. thickness. Cut with a 2½-in. cookie cutter dipped in flour. Place 1 in. apart on ungreased baking sheets. Bake until edges begin to brown, 8-10 minutes. Cool for 2 minutes before removing from pans to wire racks to cool completely. Decorate as desired.

1 COOKIE: 79 cal., 5g fat (3g sat. fat), 16mg chol., 67mg sod., 9g carb. (4g sugars, 0 fiber), 1g pro.

Memorable Easter Menu

Shrimp & Cucumber Canapes

Mustard & Cranberry Glazed Ham

Passover Popovers

Roasted Carrots with Thyme

Bibb Lettuce with
Roasted Red Onions

Potatoes Lyonnaise

Tuscan-Style Roasted Asparagus

Raspberry & White
Chocolate Cheesecake

MUSTARD & CRANBERRY GLAZED HAM

My delicious glaze uses only four ingredients. It's a simple way to
ensure your ham will be the showstopper on your table.

—Nella Parker, Hersey, MI

PREP: 15 MIN. • BAKE: 1 HOUR 50 MIN. + STANDING • MAKES: 12 SERVINGS (4 CUPS SAUCE)

1   fully cooked bone-in
    ham (6 to 8 lbs.)
    Whole cloves
3   cans (14 oz. each)
    jellied or whole-berry
    cranberry sauce
1½ cups packed brown sugar
1½ cups dry red wine
    or chicken broth
3   Tbsp. Dijon mustard

1. Preheat oven to 325°. Place ham on a rack in a shallow
roasting pan. If desired, score the surface of the ham, making
diamond shapes ½ in. deep. Insert cloves into the surface.
Loosely cover ham with foil; bake 1½ hours.

2. In a large saucepan, combine cranberry sauce, brown sugar
and wine. Bring to a boil. Reduce heat; simmer, uncovered,
10 minutes or until slightly thickened. Remove from the heat;
whisk in mustard.

3. Pour 2 cups of the cranberry mixture over the ham. Bake
20-30 minutes longer or until a thermometer reads 140°. Let
stand 10 minutes before slicing. Serve with remaining sauce.

4 OZ. COOKED HAM WITH ⅓ CUP SAUCE: 449 cal., 6g fat (2g sat. fat),
99mg chol., 1310mg sod., 65g carb. (51g sugars, 1g fiber), 33g pro.

KITCHEN TIP: Save yourself some time by preparing the glaze
a day early and storing it in the refrigerator until you're ready
to prepare the ham.

PASSOVER POPOVERS

Popovers have an important role at the Passover table as a substitute
for bread. When puffed and golden brown, they're ready to share.

—*Gloria Mezikofsky, Wakefield, MA*

PREP: 25 MIN. • BAKE: 20 MIN. + STANDING • MAKES: 1 DOZEN

1 cup water
½ cup safflower oil
⅛ to ¼ tsp. salt
1 cup matzo cake meal
7 large eggs, room
   temperature

1. Preheat oven to 450°. Generously grease 12 muffin cups. In
a large saucepan, bring water, oil and salt to a rolling boil. Add
cake meal all at once and beat until blended. Remove from heat;
let stand 5 minutes.

2. Transfer mixture to a blender. Add 2 eggs; process, covered,
until blended. Continue adding 1 egg at a time and processing
until incorporated. Process until the mixture is smooth, about
2 minutes longer.

3. Fill prepared muffin cups three-fourths full. Bake until puffed,
very firm and golden brown, 18-22 minutes. Turn off the oven
(do not open oven door); leave popovers in oven 10 minutes.
Immediately remove popovers from pan to a wire rack. Serve
popovers hot.

NOTE: This recipe was tested with Manischewitz cake meal. Look
for it in the baking aisle or kosher foods section.

1 POPOVER: 174 cal., 12g fat (2g sat. fat), 109mg chol., 66mg sod.,
11g carb. (0 sugars, 0 fiber), 5g pro.

BUNNY
NAPKIN FOLD
Easter Bunny-shaped napkins with Easter eggs nestled inside make adorable accents to your place settings. Make sure to use starched cloth square napkins and hard-boiled eggs. Plastic eggs work, too. Tie the napkin with pretty ribbon or twine.

ROASTED CARROTS WITH THYME

Cutting the carrots lengthwise makes this dish look extra pretty.

—Deirdre Cox, Kansas City, MO

TAKES: 30 MIN. • **MAKES:** 4 SERVINGS

1 lb. medium carrots, peeled and halved lengthwise
2 tsp. minced fresh thyme or ½ tsp. dried thyme
2 tsp. canola oil
1 tsp. honey
¼ tsp. salt

Preheat oven to 400°. Place the carrots in a greased 15x10x1-in. baking pan. In a small bowl, mix thyme, oil, honey and salt; brush over carrots. Roast until tender, 20-25 minutes.

1 SERVING: 73 cal., 3g fat (0 sat. fat), 0 chol., 226mg sod., 12g carb. (7g sugars, 3g fiber), 1g pro.
DIABETIC EXCHANGES: 1 vegetable, ½ fat.

BIBB LETTUCE WITH ROASTED RED ONIONS

Forget boring tossed salads! This side will have your guests asking for the recipe.
Top with bacon, or substitute feta for Gorgonzola for a change of taste.

—*Josh Carter, Birmingham, AL*

PREP: 25 MIN. • BAKE: 20 MIN. • MAKES: 8 SERVINGS

2 medium red onions,
   cut into ¼-in. wedges
1 Tbsp. olive oil
⅛ tsp. salt
⅛ tsp. pepper
1⅓ cups balsamic vinegar
6 Tbsp. orange juice
4 heads Boston or
   Bibb lettuce, halved
   lengthwise
½ cup crumbled
   Gorgonzola cheese
   Toasted chopped
   walnuts, optional

1. Preheat oven to 400°. Place onions on a foil-lined baking sheet. Drizzle with oil. Sprinkle with salt and pepper; toss to coat. Roast until tender, 20-25 minutes, stirring occasionally.

2. In a small saucepan, combine vinegar and juice. Bring to a boil; cook until reduced by half, 8-10 minutes.

3. Top lettuce halves with roasted onions. Drizzle with sauce and top with cheese. Sprinkle with additional black pepper and, if desired, chopped walnuts.

1 SERVING: 101 cal., 4g fat (2g sat. fat), 6mg chol., 135mg sod., 15g carb. (13g sugars, 1g fiber), 2g pro.
DIABETIC EXCHANGES: 2 vegetable, 1 fat.

SHRIMP & CUCUMBER CANAPES

These cute stacks really stand out in an appetizer buffet.
Tasty, cool and crunchy, they come together in a snap.

—*Ashley Nochlin, Port St. Lucie, FL*

TAKES: 25 MIN. • MAKES: 2 DOZEN

½ cup ketchup
4 tsp. Creole seasoning, divided
1 Tbsp. finely chopped onion
1 Tbsp. finely chopped green pepper
1 Tbsp. finely chopped celery
¼ tsp. hot pepper sauce
1 pkg. (8 oz.) cream cheese, softened
24 English cucumber slices
24 peeled and deveined cooked medium shrimp
2 Tbsp. minced fresh parsley

1. For cocktail sauce, in a small bowl, combine the ketchup, 2 tsp. Creole seasoning, onion, green pepper, celery and pepper sauce. In another bowl, combine cream cheese and remaining Creole seasoning.

2. Spread or pipe the cream cheese mixture onto cucumber slices. Top each with a shrimp and cocktail sauce. Sprinkle with parsley.

1 CANAPE: 50 cal., 3g fat (2g sat. fat), 26mg chol., 218mg sod., 2g carb. (1g sugars, 0 fiber), 3g pro.

KITCHEN TIP: If you don't have Creole seasoning in your cupboard, you can make your own using ¼ tsp. each salt, garlic powder and paprika, and a pinch each of dried thyme, ground cumin and cayenne pepper.

POTATOES LYONNAISE

Potatoes lyonnaise is a classic side dish I learned to make in culinary school. I keep switching up the herbs to give it a different flavor. It is very simple to make and couldn't be more comforting. It's fantastic for casual dinners, but also elegant enough for the special meals.

—*James Schend, Pleasant Prairie, WI*

PREP: 10 MIN. • **COOK:** 25 MIN. • **MAKES:** 6 SERVINGS

4 medium russet potatoes (about 1½ lbs.), peeled and thinly sliced
1 tsp. salt
6 Tbsp. butter, divided
1 small onion, halved and thinly sliced
1 tsp. minced fresh rosemary
½ tsp. pepper

SERVE IT WITH:
Salmon with Horseradish Pistachio Crust, Page 85

1. In a large saucepan or Dutch oven, combine potatoes, salt and enough cold water to cover by 1 in. Bring to a boil; reduce heat and simmer until potatoes are slightly cooked but still al dente, 3-4 minutes. Drain.

2. Meanwhile, in a large skillet, melt 3 Tbsp. butter over medium heat. Add onion; cook, stirring frequently, until golden brown, 10-12 minutes. Remove onion; set aside. In same skillet, melt remaining 3 Tbsp. butter. Add the potatoes; cook, stirring occasionally, until potatoes are golden brown, 8-10 minutes. Add onions, rosemary and pepper; toss to combine. Cook until heated through.

⅔ CUP: 190 cal., 12g fat (7g sat. fat), 31mg chol., 134mg sod., 21g carb. (2g sugars, 2g fiber), 2g pro.

TUSCAN-STYLE ROASTED ASPARAGUS

This is especially wonderful when locally grown asparagus is in season,
and it's so easy for celebrations because you can serve it hot or cold.
—*Jannine Fisk, Malden, MA*

PREP: 20 MIN. • BAKE: 15 MIN. • MAKES: 8 SERVINGS

1½ lbs. fresh asparagus,
    trimmed
1½ cups grape
    tomatoes, halved
3 Tbsp. pine nuts
3 Tbsp. olive oil, divided
2 garlic cloves, minced
1 tsp. kosher salt
½ tsp. pepper
1 Tbsp. lemon juice
⅓ cup grated Parmesan
    cheese
1 tsp. grated lemon zest

1. Preheat oven to 400°. Place the asparagus, tomatoes and
pine nuts on a foil-lined 15x10x1-in. baking pan. Mix 2 Tbsp.
oil, garlic, salt and pepper; add to asparagus and toss to coat.

2. Bake 15-20 minutes or just until asparagus is tender. Drizzle
with remaining oil and the lemon juice; sprinkle with cheese and
lemon zest. Toss to combine.

1 SERVING: 95 cal., 8g fat (2g sat. fat), 3mg chol., 294mg sod.,
4g carb. (2g sugars, 1g fiber), 3g pro. **DIABETIC EXCHANGES:** 1½ fat,
1 vegetable.

KITCHEN TIP: Common olive oil works better for cooking at high
heat than virgin or extra virgin oil. These higher grades have ideal
flavor for cold foods, but they smoke at lower temperatures.

RASPBERRY & WHITE CHOCOLATE CHEESECAKE

*My mom makes this cheesecake a lot because it's so good and really pretty.
She calls it a go-to recipe. Someday I'll try to make it myself.*

—Peggy Roos, Minneapolis, MN

PREP: 40 MIN. • **BAKE:** 1¾ HOURS + CHILLING • **MAKES:** 16 SERVINGS

1　pkg. (10 oz.)
　　frozen sweetened
　　raspberries, thawed
1　Tbsp. cornstarch

CRUST
1　cup all-purpose flour
2　Tbsp. sugar
½　cup cold butter

FILLING
4　pkg. (8 oz. each) cream
　　cheese, softened
1½　cups sugar
1¼　cups heavy
　　whipping cream
2　tsp. vanilla extract
2　large eggs, room
　　temperature,
　　lightly beaten
12　oz. white baking
　　chocolate, melted
　　and cooled

**SERVE
IT WITH:**
Grilled Lemon Chicken,
Page 101

1. In a small saucepan, mix raspberries and cornstarch until blended. Bring to a boil; cook and stir 1-2 minutes or until thickened. Press through a fine-mesh strainer into a bowl; discard seeds. Cool completely.

2. Preheat oven to 350°. Place a greased 9-in. springform pan on a double thickness of heavy-duty foil (about 18 in. square). Wrap foil securely around pan.

3. For crust, in a small bowl, mix flour and sugar. Cut in butter until crumbly. Press onto bottom of prepared pan. Place pan on a baking sheet. Bake 20-25 minutes or until golden brown. Cool on a wire rack. Reduce oven setting to 325°.

4. For filling, in a large bowl, beat cream cheese and sugar until smooth. Beat in cream and vanilla. Add eggs; beat on low speed just until blended. Stir in the cooled chocolate. Pour half of the mixture over crust. Spread with half of the raspberry puree. Top with remaining batter. Drop remaining puree by tablespoonfuls over top. Cut through batter with a knife to swirl.

5. Place springform pan in a larger baking pan; add 1 in. of hot water to larger pan. Bake 1¾-2 hours or until the edge of cheesecake is set and golden. (Center of cheesecake will jiggle when moved.) Remove springform pan from water bath. Cool cheesecake on a wire rack for 10 minutes. Loosen cheesecake from pan with a knife; remove foil. Cool for 1 hour longer. Refrigerate overnight. Remove rim from pan.

1 PIECE: 570 cal., 41g fat (25g sat. fat), 134mg chol., 247mg sod., 45g carb. (36g sugars, 1g fiber), 8g pro.

Happy Mother's Day

Ham Spread

Rhubarb Chutney

Lemon Risotto with Broccoli

Chilled Asparagus
with Basil Cream

Roast Leg of Lamb

Rose & Raspberry Fool

Rhubarb Strawberry Pie

ROAST LEG OF LAMB

Lamb can be intimidating, but this simple recipe makes easy work of
a springtime favorite. The herb mixture provides tons of flavor.
—*Sharon Cusson, Augusta, ME*

PREP: 5 MIN. • BAKE: 2 HOURS + STANDING • MAKES: 10 SERVINGS

1   bone-in leg of lamb
     (6 to 8 lbs.), trimmed
2   garlic cloves, minced
½   tsp. dried thyme
½   tsp. dried marjoram
½   tsp. dried oregano
¼   tsp. salt
⅛   tsp. pepper
1   tsp. canola oil

1. Preheat oven to 325°. Place lamb on a rack in a shallow roasting pan, fat side up. Cut 12-14 slits ½ in. deep in roast. Combine garlic, thyme, marjoram, oregano, salt and pepper; spoon 2 tsp. into the slits. Brush roast with oil; rub with the remaining herb mixture.

2. Bake, uncovered, until meat reaches desired doneness (for medium-rare, a thermometer should read 135°; medium, 140°; medium-well, 145°), 2-2½ hours. Let meat stand 15 minutes before slicing.

5 OZ. COOKED LAMB: 227 cal., 9g fat (4g sat. fat), 122mg chol., 114mg sod., 0 carb. (0 sugars, 0 fiber), 34g pro. **DIABETIC EXCHANGES:** 5 lean meat.

TOMATO TULIPS

Kids can help pick, stuff and arrange this edible Mom's Day bouquet.

INGREDIENTS
☐ 1 pint grape tomatoes

☐ 3 oz. cream cheese, softened

☐ ¼ cup ranch salad dressing

☐ 2 Tbsp. thinly sliced green onion

☐ 2 Tbsp. finely chopped water chestnuts

☐ 2 Tbsp. finely chopped walnuts

☐ Whole chives, optional

STEP 1
Using a knife, make an "X" in the top of each tomato, cutting two-thirds of the way to the bottom. Scoop out pulp with the tip of a knife. Drain tomatoes, upside down, on a paper towel.

STEP 2
Combine next 5 ingredients in a small bowl. Stuff tomatoes with filling. Keep refrigerated until serving time. If desired, garnish with chives for flower stems.

LEMON RISOTTO WITH BROCCOLI

Serve this rich and creamy side dish at your next dinner party. It's a tasty alternative to potatoes.

—Judy Grebetz, Racine, WI

PREP: 25 MIN. • **COOK:** 30 MIN. • **MAKES:** 8 SERVINGS

3 cans (14½ oz. each) reduced-sodium chicken broth
1 Tbsp. olive oil
1 small onion, finely chopped
1½ cups uncooked arborio rice
2 tsp. grated lemon zest
½ cup dry white wine or additional reduced-sodium chicken broth
3 cups chopped fresh broccoli
⅓ cup grated Parmesan cheese
1 Tbsp. lemon juice
2 tsp. minced fresh thyme

1. In a large saucepan, bring broth to a simmer; keep hot. In another large saucepan heat oil over medium heat. Add onion; cook and stir until tender, 3-5 minutes. Add rice and lemon zest; cook and stir until rice is coated, 1-2 minutes.

2. Stir in wine. Reduce heat to maintain a simmer; cook and stir until wine is absorbed. Add hot broth, ½ cup at a time, cooking and stirring until broth has been absorbed after each addition, adding broccoli after half the broth has been added. Cook until rice is tender but firm to the bite, and risotto is creamy. Remove from heat; stir in cheese and lemon juice. Sprinkle with thyme. Serve immediately.

⅔ CUP: 201 cal., 3g fat (1g sat. fat), 3mg chol., 460mg sod., 35g carb. (2g sugars, 2g fiber), 7g pro. **DIABETIC EXCHANGES:** 2 starch, ½ fat.

HAM SPREAD

My husband, Keith, and I enjoy simple recipes when entertaining. We share the cooking responsibilities and make this ham spread when our kids and grandkids are home for different holidays.

—*Marilyn Strahm, Lincoln, NE*

PREP: 15 MIN. + CHILLING • MAKES: 2½ CUPS

1 pkg. (8 oz.) cream
  cheese, softened
¼ cup mayonnaise
¼ cup ranch salad dressing
2 Tbsp. minced
  fresh parsley
1 tsp. finely chopped onion
½ tsp. ground mustard
½ tsp. hot pepper
  sauce, optional
2 cups finely chopped
  fully cooked ham
⅓ cup chopped pecans
  Assorted crackers

1. In a small mixing bowl, combine cream cheese, mayonnaise, salad dressing, parsley, onion, mustard and, if desired, pepper sauce until smooth. Stir in ham. (Mixture will be soft.) Line a 3-cup bowl with plastic wrap. Spoon ham mixture into bowl; cover and refrigerate at least 8 hours or overnight.

2. Invert ham mixture onto a serving plate; discard plastic wrap. Press pecans onto surface of ham mixture. Serve ham spread with crackers.

2 TBSP.: 100 cal., 9g fat (3g sat. fat), 20mg chol., 248mg sod., 1g carb. (1g sugars, 0 fiber), 4g pro.

KITCHEN TIP: It can take almost an hour for a block of cold cream cheese to soften when removed from the refrigerator and placed on the countertop. To speed up the process, cut the block into 1-in. cubes. Transfer the cubes to a plate or food-safe surface and cover with plastic wrap. Let the cubes sit for up to 30 minutes to fully soften.

ROSE & RASPBERRY FOOL

I came up with this recipe when I was going through a floral phase, putting rose or lavender in everything. This dessert is easy to make, but elegant enough to serve company.

—*Carolyn Eskew, Dayton, OH*

PREP: 15 MIN. + CHILLING • MAKES: 8 SERVINGS

2 cups fresh or frozen
  raspberries
6 Tbsp. sugar, divided
1½ cups heavy
  whipping cream
1 tsp. rose water
  Fresh mint leaves

1. In a small bowl, lightly crush raspberries and 2 Tbsp. sugar. Cover and refrigerate 1-2 hours.

2. In a large bowl, beat cream until it begins to thicken. Add remaining 4 Tbsp. sugar and rose water; beat until soft peaks form. Gently fold in raspberry mixture. Spoon into dessert dishes. Garnish with mint leaves and, if desired, additional berries. Serve immediately.

½ **CUP:** 206 cal., 16g fat (10g sat. fat), 51mg chol., 13mg sod., 14g carb. (12g sugars, 2g fiber), 2g pro.

MAKE IT LAST
Rinse the inside of the artichoke with lemon juice to keep the flowers fresher longer.

CHILLED ASPARAGUS WITH BASIL CREAM

This recipe is an all-time family favorite that has been served at many of our holiday meals. I like it because it's simple and can be prepared ahead of time.

—*Melissa Puccetti, Rohnert Park, CA*

TAKES: 20 MIN. • **MAKES:** 8 SERVINGS

2 lbs. fresh asparagus, trimmed
1 cup mayonnaise
¼ cup heavy whipping cream
4 Tbsp. minced fresh basil, divided
2 garlic cloves, peeled and halved
½ tsp. salt
¼ tsp. pepper
2 Tbsp. pine nuts, toasted
1 Tbsp. grated lemon zest

1. In a large saucepan, bring 8 cups water to a boil. Add half the asparagus; cook, uncovered, 2-4 minutes or until just crisp-tender. Remove asparagus and immediately drop into ice water. Drain and pat dry. Repeat with remaining asparagus. Arrange on a serving platter.

2. Place mayonnaise, cream, 3 Tbsp. basil, garlic, salt and pepper in a food processor; cover and process until blended. Spoon over asparagus. Garnish with pine nuts, lemon zest and remaining 1 Tbsp. basil.

1 SERVING: 235 cal., 24g fat (5g sat. fat), 10mg chol., 296mg sod., 3g carb. (1g sugars, 1g fiber), 2g pro.

GARDEN BEAUTY

Take springtime veggies from garden to table with these fresh centerpiece ideas (shown on opposite page).

ARTICHOKE VASE
Using a chef's knife, cut off an artichoke's stem and level its base. Using a serrated knife, cut off the top fourth of the artichoke. Open the leaves slightly by gently pushing them outward. Use a melon baller to scoop out the interior of the artichoke just down to its base, deep enough to hold the stems of a small bouquet of flowers. Add the bouquet and adjust arrangement as needed.

RADISH CENTERPIECE
Cut radish leaves off at the stem base. Place radishes in a glass hurricane vase and arrange as desired. Mix cold water with a couple of drops of dish soap, then pour the mixture around the radishes to fill the vase (the soap will help keep the radish leaves from wilting). Arrange radish leaves at the top of the vase to desired fullness.

ASPARAGUS-WRAPPED CANDLE
Trim asparagus so tips reach about ½ inch below the top of a pillar candle. Place stalks around the candle and secure with a rubber band at the center. Cut two pieces of raffia string, ensuring they're long enough to create 2 inches of overhang when tied. Stack the raffia and wrap it around the asparagus, covering the rubber band. Tie and trim as needed.

RHUBARB STRAWBERRY PIE

This sweet-tart dessert is a family favorite. My husband never liked rhubarb until
he tasted this pie. Now he asks me to make it often. If rhubarb or strawberries
are not in season, you can use frozen fruit with good results.

—*Sandy Brown, Lake Worth, FL*

PREP: 15 MIN. + STANDING • **BAKE:** 40 MIN. + COOLING • **MAKES:** 8 SERVINGS

¾ **cup sugar**
¼ **cup quick-cooking
    tapioca**
3 **cups sliced fresh
    or frozen rhubarb
    (¼-in. pieces)**
3 **cups sliced fresh or
    frozen strawberries,
    thawed**
⅓ **cup orange juice**
4½ **tsp. orange
    marmalade, optional**
¼ **tsp. grated orange zest
    Dough for double-crust
    pie**

1. Preheat oven to 400°. In a large bowl, combine the sugar
and tapioca. Add the fruit; toss to coat. Gently stir in the juice,
marmalade if desired, and orange zest. Let mixture stand for
15 minutes.

2. On a lightly floured surface, roll half of dough to a ⅛-in.-thick
circle; transfer to 9-in. deep-dish pie plate. Trim to ½ in. beyond
rim of plate. Add filling.

3. Roll the remaining dough to a ⅛-in.-thick circle; cut into
¼-in.-wide strips. Arrange over filling in a lattice pattern. Trim
and seal strips to edge of bottom crust; flute edge. Cover edge
loosely with foil.

4. Bake until filling is bubbly and the rhubarb is tender,
40-50 minutes. Remove foil. Cool on a wire rack. Store in
the refrigerator.

NOTE: If using frozen rhubarb, measure rhubarb while still
frozen, then thaw completely. Drain in a colander, but do not
press liquid out.

TO MAKE DOUGH FOR DOUBLE-CRUST PIE (9 IN.): Combine 2½ cups
all-purpose flour and ½ tsp. salt; cut in 1 cup cold butter until
crumbly. Gradually add ⅓-⅔ cup ice water, tossing with a fork
until the dough holds together when pressed. Divide dough in
half. Shape each into a disk; wrap and refrigerate 1 hour.

1 PIECE: 470 cal., 23g fat (14g sat. fat), 60mg chol., 312mg sod.,
62g carb. (24g sugars, 3g fiber), 5g pro.

RHUBARB CHUTNEY

This tangy-sweet chutney is among our favorite condiments. We love it as a relish for pork or chicken, but there are so many delicious ways to enjoy it. Try it as sandwich booster, serve as a dip with tortilla chips, pair alongside curries or roasted veggies, or slather it on party crostini.

—Jan Paterson, Anchorage, AK

TAKES: 20 MIN. • MAKES: ABOUT 3 CUPS

¾ cup sugar
⅓ cup cider vinegar
1 Tbsp. minced garlic
¾ tsp. ground ginger
½ tsp. ground cumin
½ tsp. ground cinnamon
¼ tsp. crushed red
   pepper flakes
⅛ to ¼ tsp. ground cloves
4 cups coarsely chopped
   fresh or frozen
   rhubarb, thawed
½ cup chopped red onion
⅓ cup golden raisins
1 tsp. red food
   coloring, optional

1. In a large saucepan, combine the sugar, vinegar, garlic, ginger, cumin, cinnamon, red pepper flakes and cloves. Bring to a boil. Reduce heat; simmer, uncovered, until sugar is dissolved, about 2 minutes.

2. Add the rhubarb, onion and raisins. Cook and stir over medium heat until rhubarb is tender and mixture is slightly thickened, 5-10 minutes. Stir in food coloring if desired. Cool completely. Store in the refrigerator.

NOTE: If using frozen rhubarb, measure rhubarb while still frozen, then thaw completely. Drain in a colander, but do not press liquid out.

¼ CUP: 75 cal., 0 fat (0 sat. fat), 0 chol., 3mg sod., 19g carb. (17g sugars, 1g fiber), 1g pro.

KITCHEN TIP: During the simmering process, the vinegar will create a pungent aroma. So be sure you're working in a well-ventilated area.

A Special Sunday Dinner

Salmon with Horseradish
Pistachio Crust

···

Palmiers

···

Shrimp Salad
with Wine Vinaigrette

···

Zesty Mediterranean
Potato Salad

···

Green Beans with
Creamy Pistachio Sauce

···

Chocolate Chiffon Cake

···

Slow-Cooker Tequila
Poached Pears

SALMON WITH HORSERADISH PISTACHIO CRUST

Impress everyone at your table with this elegant but easy salmon. Feel free to switch up the ingredients to suit your tastes. You can substitute scallions for the shallots or try almonds or pecans instead of pistachios. The nutty coating also plays well with chicken and pork.

—Linda Press Wolfe, Cross River, NY

TAKES: 30 MIN. • **MAKES:** 6 SERVINGS

- 6 salmon fillets (4 oz. each)
- ⅓ cup sour cream
- ⅔ cup dry bread crumbs
- ⅔ cup chopped pistachios
- ½ cup minced shallots
- 2 Tbsp. olive oil
- 1 to 2 Tbsp. prepared horseradish
- 1 Tbsp. snipped fresh dill or 1 tsp. dill weed
- ½ tsp. grated lemon or orange zest
- ¼ tsp. crushed red pepper flakes
- 1 garlic clove, minced

Preheat oven to 350°. Place salmon, skin side down, in an ungreased 15x10x1-in. baking pan. Spread sour cream over each fillet. Combine remaining ingredients. Pat crumb-nut mixture onto tops of salmon fillets, pressing to help coating adhere. Bake until fish just begins to flake easily with a fork, 12-15 minutes.

1 SALMON FILLET: 376 cal., 25g fat (5g sat. fat), 60mg chol., 219mg sod., 15g carb. (3g sugars, 2g fiber), 24g pro. **DIABETIC EXCHANGES:** 3 lean meat, 2 fat.

KITCHEN TIP: Make sure to use plain horseradish, not horseradish sauce or creamed horseradish.

PALMIERS

It takes just two ingredients to make these impressive but easy-to-do
French pastries, which are often called palm leaves.
—Taste of Home *Test Kitchen*

PREP: 20 MIN. + FREEZING • **BAKE:** 10 MIN. + COOLING • **MAKES:** 2 DOZEN

1 cup sugar, divided
1 sheet frozen puff
   pastry, thawed

1. Preheat oven to 425°. Sprinkle a surface with ¼ cup sugar; unfold puff pastry sheet on surface. Sprinkle with 2 Tbsp. sugar. Roll into a 14x10-in. rectangle. Sprinkle with ½ cup sugar to within ½ in. of edges. Lightly press into pastry.

2. With a knife, very lightly score a line crosswise across the middle of the pastry. Starting at a short side, roll up jelly-roll style, stopping at the score mark in the middle. Starting at the other side, roll up pastry jelly-roll style to score mark. Freeze until firm, 20-30 minutes. Cut into ⅜-in. slices.

3. Place cut side up 2 in. apart on parchment-lined baking sheets; sprinkle lightly with 1 Tbsp. sugar. Bake for 8 minutes. Turn pastries over and sprinkle with remaining sugar. Bake until golden brown and glazed, about 3 minutes longer. Remove to wire racks to cool completely. Store in airtight containers.

1 PASTRY: 83 cal., 3g fat (1g sat. fat), 0mg chol., 34mg sod., 14g carb. (8g sugars, 1g fiber), 1g pro.

SHRIMP SALAD WITH WINE VINAIGRETTE

This veggie and seafood salad is light and versatile—you can use whatever vegetables you prefer.

—Cecilia Flowers, Nashville, NC

PREP: 45 MIN. • COOK: 35 MIN. • MAKES: 5 SERVINGS

4 large artichokes
1 lb. fresh asparagus, trimmed
1 cup chopped fresh cauliflower
1 cup fresh broccoli florets
½ cup dry red wine
2 shallots, finely chopped, divided
¼ cup olive oil
¼ cup red wine vinegar
2 tsp. Dijon mustard
¼ tsp. salt
¼ tsp. pepper
6 cups spring mix salad greens
1 bunch watercress
20 large shrimp, cooked, peeled and deveined
1 small fennel bulb, thinly sliced, fronds reserved
½ cup julienned sweet red pepper

1. With a sharp knife, level the bottom of each artichoke and cut 1 in. from the top. With kitchen scissors, snip off tips of outer leaves. Place in a steamer basket in a large saucepan over 1 in. of water. Bring to a boil; cover and steam until leaves near the center pull out easily, 20-25 minutes. Add the asparagus, cauliflower and broccoli ; cover and cook until crisp-tender, 3-4 minutes. Drain. With a spoon, carefully remove and discard fuzzy centers of the artichokes. Thinly slice artichoke hearts.

2. Meanwhile, in a small saucepan, combine wine and 1 shallot. Bring to a boil; cook until liquid is reduced to about 2 Tbsp.. In a small bowl, whisk the oil, vinegar, wine mixture, mustard, salt, pepper and remaining shallot; set aside.

3. Place salad greens and watercress on a large platter. Top with the cooked vegetables, shrimp, fennel, red pepper and artichoke slices. Drizzle with dressing and sprinkle with reserved fennel fronds.

2 CUPS: 277 cal., 12g fat (2g sat. fat), 79mg chol., 446mg sod., 27g carb. (7g sugars, 11g fiber), 19g pro. **DIABETIC EXCHANGES:** 2 starch, 2 lean meat, 2 fat.

ZESTY MEDITERRANEAN POTATO SALAD

I love this recipe that incorporates many of the vegetables I plant in my
garden. The dressing is light and fresh—perfect for a picnic or barbecue.

—*Terri Crandall, Gardnerville, NV*

PREP: 25 MIN. • **COOK:** 15 MIN. + CHILLING • **MAKES:** 8 SERVINGS

4 large Yukon Gold
  potatoes, peeled
  and cubed
1½ tsp. salt, divided
½ cup olive oil
¼ cup lemon juice
½ tsp. pepper
⅛ tsp. crushed red
  pepper flakes
1 medium sweet red
  pepper, finely chopped
½ small red onion,
  finely chopped
⅓ cup Greek olives,
  pitted and chopped
4 bacon strips, cooked
  and crumbled
½ cup crumbled feta cheese
¼ cup loosely packed
  basil leaves, torn

1. Place potatoes in a large saucepan; add water to cover. Add
1 tsp. salt. Bring to a boil. Reduce heat; cook, uncovered, until
tender, 8-10 minutes. Drain and place in a large bowl.

2. In a small bowl, whisk olive oil, lemon juice, remaining salt,
pepper and red pepper flakes until blended. Spoon over potato
mixture; toss to coat. Refrigerate, covered, until chilled, about
1 hour. Just before serving, add sweet red pepper, onion, olives
and bacon to potatoes. Sprinkle with feta and basil.

¾ CUP: 341 cal., 18g fat (3g sat. fat), 8mg chol., 685mg sod.,
40g carb. (4g sugars, 3g fiber), 6g pro.

KITCHEN TIP: Remember this salad the next time you're looking
for a change-of-pace addition to a picnic.

GREEN BEANS WITH CREAMY PISTACHIO SAUCE

I was asked to bring vegetables for a party and wasn't feeling inspired until I remembered Mom served them with butter and evaporated milk. I love pistachios, so I added those instead of almonds. Everybody wanted the recipe, and I was really pleased—very little work and lots of happy family and friends!

—*Loretta Ouellette, Pompano Beach, FL*

TAKES: 30 MIN. • MAKES: 10 SERVINGS

2 lbs. fresh green beans, trimmed
1 tsp. salt
½ cup butter, cubed
½ cup pistachios, coarsely chopped
1 cup evaporated milk
Salt and pepper to taste

SERVE
IT WITH:
All-Day Brisket with Potatoes,
Page 102

1. Place green beans and salt in a Dutch oven; add water to cover. Bring to a boil. Cook, uncovered, until tender, stirring occasionally, 5-8 minutes. Drain and remove from pan.

2. In the same pan, melt cubed butter over medium heat. Add pistachios; cook and stir until pistachios begin to brown, about 1-2 minutes. Stir in evaporated milk; bring to a boil. Cook until sauce is slightly thickened, 2-4 minutes. Add green beans; heat through, stirring to coat with sauce. Season with salt and pepper to taste.

¾ CUP: 177 cal., 14g fat (7g sat. fat), 32mg chol., 365mg sod., 11g carb. (5g sugars, 4g fiber), 5g pro.

CHOCOLATE CHIFFON CAKE

If you want to offer family and friends a dessert that really stands out from the rest, this is the cake to make. The beautiful tall, rich sponge cake is drizzled with a succulent chocolate glaze.

—Erma Fox, Memphis, MO

PREP: 25 MIN. + COOLING • **BAKE:** 1 HOUR + COOLING • **MAKES:** 20 SERVINGS

7 large eggs, separated
½ cup baking cocoa
¾ cup boiling water
1¾ cups cake flour
1¾ cups sugar
1½ tsp. baking soda
1 tsp. salt
½ cup canola oil
2 tsp. vanilla extract
¼ tsp. cream of tartar

ICING
⅓ cup butter
2 cups confectioners' sugar
2 oz. unsweetened chocolate, melted and cooled
1½ tsp. vanilla extract
3 to 4 Tbsp. hot water
Chopped nuts, optional

1. Let eggs stand at room temperature for 30 minutes. In a bowl, combine cocoa and water until smooth; cool for 20 minutes. In a large bowl, combine flour, sugar, baking soda and salt. In a bowl, whisk the egg yolks, oil and vanilla; add to dry ingredients along with the cocoa mixture. Beat until well blended. In another large bowl and with clean beaters, beat egg whites and cream of tartar on high speed until stiff peaks form. Gradually fold into egg yolk mixture.

2. Gently spoon batter into an ungreased 10-in. tube pan. Cut through the batter with a knife to remove air pockets. Bake on lowest rack at 325° for 60-65 minutes or until top springs back when lightly touched. Immediately invert pan; cool completely. Run a knife around side and center tube of pan. Invert cake onto a serving plate.

3. For icing, melt butter in a saucepan. Remove from the heat; stir in the confectioners' sugar, chocolate, vanilla and water. Drizzle over cake. Sprinkle with nuts if desired.

1 PIECE: 268 cal., 11g fat (3g sat. fat), 73mg chol., 262mg sod., 40g carb. (30g sugars, 1g fiber), 4g pro.

CAREFULLY COOLING A CHIFFON CAKE

Cool chiffon cake upside down in the pan. Otherwise, it will collapse and flatten. If your tube pan has legs, invert it onto its legs until the cake is completely cool. If your tube pan does not have legs, gently place the pan over a funnel or the neck of a narrow bottle until cake is completely cool.

SLOW-COOKER TEQUILA POACHED PEARS

It's an unusual dessert to make with tequila, but it is deliciously refreshing with fresh pears and mint. Bring out this creative sweet when you want to impress dinner guests.

—*Nancy Heishman, Las Vegas, NV*

PREP: 20 MIN. • COOK: 4 HOURS 20 MIN. • MAKES: 8 SERVINGS

2 cups water
1 can (11.3 oz.) pear nectar
1 cup tequila
½ cup sugar
2 Tbsp. lime juice
2 tsp. grated lime zest
1 cinnamon stick (3 in.)
¼ tsp. ground nutmeg
8 whole Anjou
   pears, peeled
   Sweetened whipped
   cream, optional
   Fresh mint leaves

1. In a large saucepan, combine the first 8 ingredients. Bring to a boil over medium-high heat; boil 2 minutes, stirring constantly.

2. Place pears in a 4- or 5-qt. slow cooker; add liquid. Cook, covered, on low until tender, 4-5 hours. Remove cinnamon stick and discard. Pour 3 cups cooking liquid in a small saucepan. Bring to a boil; cook, uncovered, until liquid is reduced to 1 cup, about 20 minutes.

3. Halve pears lengthwise and core them. Serve with sauce, whipped cream if desired, and mint leaves.

1 PEAR WITH 2 TBSP. SAUCE: 155 cal., 0 fat (0 sat. fat), 0 chol., 3mg sod., 40g carb. (30g sugars, 6g fiber), 1g pro.

SUMMER PARTIES

Backyard Bash

Grilled Lemon Chicken

All-Day Brisket with Potatoes

Ghost Pepper
Popcorn Cornbread

BLT Macaroni Salad

Sweet & Spicy Baked Beans

Southern Potato Salad

Air-Fryer Spicy Ginger
Beef Skewers

Golden Peach Pie

GRILLED LEMON CHICKEN

My chicken gets its subtle bit of pucker from lemonade concentrate. So simple, so sweet!
—Linda Nilsen, Anoka, MN

PREP: 5 MIN. • **GRILL:** 40 MIN. • **MAKES:** 12 SERVINGS

¾ cup thawed lemonade
   concentrate
⅓ cup soy sauce
1 garlic clove, minced
1 tsp. seasoned salt
½ tsp. celery salt
⅛ tsp. garlic powder
2 broiler/fryer chickens
   (3 to 3½ lbs. each), cut up

1. In a bowl, whisk the first 6 ingredients until combined. Pour half into a shallow glass dish. Cover and refrigerate remaining lemonade mixture.

2. Dip chicken into lemonade mixture, turning to coat; discard lemonade mixture. Grill chicken, covered, over medium heat for 30 minutes, turning occasionally. Brush with the reserved lemonade mixture. Grill chicken 10-20 minutes longer, brushing frequently, until a thermometer reads 165°.

5 OZ. COOKED CHICKEN: 320 cal., 17g fat (5g sat. fat), 104mg chol., 504mg sod., 6g carb. (5g sugars, 0 fiber), 34g pro.

ALL-DAY BRISKET WITH POTATOES

I think the slow cooker was invented with brisket in mind. This sweet and savory version is perfection itself, because it melts in your mouth. For this recipe, it's important to buy first-cut or flat-cut brisket, which has far less fat than other cuts.

—Lana Gryga, Glen Flora, WI

PREP: 30 MIN. • COOK: 8 HOURS • MAKES: 8 SERVINGS

2 medium potatoes, peeled and cut into ¼-in. slices
2 celery ribs, sliced
1 fresh beef brisket (3 lbs.)
1 Tbsp. canola oil
1 large onion, sliced
2 garlic cloves, minced
1 can (12 oz.) beer
½ tsp. beef bouillon granules
¾ cup stewed tomatoes
⅓ cup tomato paste
¼ cup red wine vinegar
3 Tbsp. brown sugar
3 Tbsp. Dijon mustard
3 Tbsp. soy sauce
2 Tbsp. molasses
½ tsp. paprika
¼ tsp. salt
⅛ tsp. pepper
1 bay leaf

1. Place potatoes and celery in a 5-qt. slow cooker. Cut brisket in half. In a large skillet, brown beef in oil on all sides; transfer to slow cooker. In the same pan, saute onion until tender. Add garlic; cook 1 minute longer. Add to slow cooker.

2. Add beer and bouillon granules to skillet, stirring to loosen browned bits from pan; pour over meat. In a large bowl, combine the remaining ingredients; add to slow cooker.

3. Cover and cook on low until meat and vegetables are tender, 8-10 hours. Discard bay leaf. To serve, thinly slice across the grain.

NOTE: This is a fresh beef brisket, not corned beef.

1 SERVING: 352 cal., 9g fat (3g sat. fat), 72mg chol., 722mg sod., 25g carb. (13g sugars, 2g fiber), 38g pro.
DIABETIC EXCHANGES: 5 lean meat, 1 starch, 1 vegetable, ½ fat.

LET THE FUN TIMES RING!

To pass time until the main event, line up bottles (full or empty) of your favorite sipper in a wooden crate, and get to tossing! Mason jar rings wrapped with yarn are an easy craft—and perfect for making soft landings. Fire away!

GHOST PEPPER POPCORN CORNBREAD

I love popcorn and lots of spice and heat. I have recently been dabbling with ghost peppers and came up with this twist on classic cornbread. Add corn kernels for more texture.

—*Allison Antalek, Cuyahoga Falls, OH*

PREP: 40 MIN. • **BAKE:** 25 MIN. • **MAKES:** 8 SERVINGS

⅓ cup popcorn kernels

1 Tbsp. coconut oil
or canola oil

1 cup all-purpose flour

½ cup sugar

2 tsp. baking powder

½ tsp. baking soda

½ tsp. salt

½ tsp. crushed ghost
chile pepper or
cayenne pepper

2 large eggs, room
temperature

1½ cups 2% milk

4 Tbsp. melted
butter, divided

½ cup chopped seeded
jalapeno peppers

SERVE IT WITH:
Brined Grilled Turkey Breast,
Page 215

1. Preheat the oven to 400°. Heat a 10-in. cast-iron or other ovenproof skillet over medium heat. Add popcorn and coconut oil; cook until oil begins to sizzle. Cover and shake until popcorn stops popping, 3-4 minutes. Remove from heat.

2. Place popcorn in a food processor; process until ground. Transfer 2 cups of ground popcorn to a large bowl (save the remainder for another use). Stir in flour, sugar, baking powder, baking soda, salt and chile pepper.

3. Add eggs, milk and 2 Tbsp. butter; beat just until moistened. Stir in jalapenos. Add remaining 2 Tbsp. butter to skillet; place skillet in oven to heat. Carefully remove hot skillet from oven. Add the batter; bake until top is golden brown and a toothpick inserted in the center of cornbread comes out clean, roughly 25-30 minutes. Cut into wedges; serve warm.

1 PIECE: 241 cal., 10g fat (6g sat. fat), 65mg chol., 432mg sod., 34g carb. (15g sugars, 2g fiber), 6g pro.

KITCHEN TIP: For a fun garnish, top cornbread wedges with additional chopped jalapeno peppers or popped kernels of popcorn.

BLT MACARONI SALAD

A friend served this salad, and I just had to get the recipe. My husband loves
BLT sandwiches, so this has become a favorite of his. It's nice to serve on
hot and humid days, which we frequently get during summer here in Virginia.

—*Hamilton Myers Jr., Charlottesville, VA*

TAKES: 30 MIN. • **MAKES:** 6 SERVINGS

½ cup mayonnaise
3 Tbsp. chili sauce
2 Tbsp. lemon juice
1 tsp. sugar
3 cups cooked elbow
    macaroni
½ cup chopped
    seeded tomato
2 Tbsp. chopped
    green onions
3 cups shredded lettuce
4 bacon strips, cooked
    and crumbled

In a bowl, combine the first 4 ingredients. Add the macaroni,
tomato and onions; toss to coat. Cover and refrigerate. Just
before serving, add lettuce and bacon; toss to coat.

¾ CUP: 259 cal., 17g fat (3g sat. fat), 10mg chol., 287mg sod.,
21g carb. (4g sugars, 2g fiber), 5g pro.

KITCHEN TIP: If you're a bacon fanatic, use thick-cut bacon or add
2 extra strips to pump up the volume.

**SERVE
IT WITH:**
Spiced Pulled Pork
Sandwiches, Page 117

SWEET & SPICY BAKED BEANS

This recipe is a hit with guests and family. It's sweet, simple and delicious, and someone always asks for the recipe.

—Elliot Wesen, Arlington, TX

PREP: 15 MIN. • **BAKE:** 50 MIN. • **MAKES:** 14 SERVINGS

2 cans (28 oz. each) baked beans
1 can (20 oz.) unsweetened crushed pineapple, drained
1 cup spicy barbecue sauce
½ cup molasses
2 Tbsp. prepared mustard
½ tsp. pepper
¼ tsp. salt
1 can (6 oz.) french-fried onions, crushed, divided
5 bacon strips, cooked and crumbled, divided

1. In a large bowl, combine the first 7 ingredients. Stir in half the onions and bacon. Transfer mixture to a greased 13x9-in. baking dish.

2. Cover and bake at 350° for 45 minutes. Sprinkle with the remaining onions and bacon. Bake, uncovered, 5-10 minutes longer or until bubbly.

¾ CUP: 285 cal., 9g fat (3g sat. fat), 10mg chol., 860mg sod., 46g carb., 7g fiber, 7g pro.

BACKYARD DOMINOES

Bring the fun of a classic game outdoors with these oversized lawn dominoes.

MATERIALS
☐ Three 1x12-in. boards (two 6 ft. in length, one 4 ft. in length)
☐ Stain
☐ White paint
☐ White paint marker
☐ Polycrylic finish
☐ Miter saw
☐ Rag or foam brush
☐ Paintbrush

STEP 1
Using a miter saw, cut boards to 28 pieces sized 5½ in. each.

STEP 2
Apply stain to pieces with rag or foam brush. Dry thoroughly.

STEP 3
Paint a white line horizontally across the center of each board. Use white paint marker to apply appropriate dots to pieces. Dry boards thoroughly.

STEP 4
Apply polycrylic finish to all pieces to seal. Dry thoroughly.

SOUTHERN POTATO SALAD

This potato salad with a southern twist is perfect for a church supper or potluck. The pickles add an extra sweetness.

—Gene Pitts, Wilsonville, AL

PREP: 30 MIN. + CHILLING • MAKES: 8 SERVINGS

5 medium potatoes, peeled and cubed
6 hard-boiled large eggs, chopped
½ cup thinly sliced green onions
¼ cup chopped sweet pickles
1 tsp. prepared mustard
1 tsp. celery seed
1 cup mayonnaise
Salt and pepper to taste

Place potatoes in a large saucepan; add water to cover. Bring to a boil. Reduce heat; cook, uncovered, 10-15 minutes or until tender. Drain; refrigerate until cold. Add the eggs, green onions and pickles; toss well. Stir in prepared mustard, celery seed and mayonnaise. Season with salt and pepper; mix well. Refrigerate until serving.

¾ CUP: 377 cal., 26g fat (4g sat. fat), 169mg chol., 275mg sod., 28g carb. (5g sugars, 2g fiber), 8g pro.

KITCHEN TIP: Many potato salad recipes instruct to peel the potatoes before boiling. This is a matter of personal preference. Some cooks leave them on for added color, texture and nutrients. Just scrub them well under cold-running water to make sure they're absolutely clean before cooking.

AIR-FRYER SPICY GINGER BEEF SKEWERS

My family loves the flavors of these zippy kabobs. I usually grill them
outside, but if it's cold or rainy, I cook them in my air fryer.

—Jasey McBurnett, Rock Springs, WY

PREP: 20 MIN. + MARINATING • **COOK:** 5 MIN. • **MAKES:** 6 SERVINGS

1 **beef flank steak (1½ lbs.)**
1 **cup rice vinegar**
1 **cup soy sauce**
¼ **cup packed brown sugar**
2 **Tbsp. minced fresh
   gingerroot**
6 **garlic cloves, minced**
3 **tsp. sesame oil**
2 **tsp. Sriracha chili sauce
   or 1 tsp. hot pepper sauce**
½ **tsp. cornstarch
   Optional: Sesame seeds
   and thinly sliced green
   onions**

1. Cut beef into ¼-in.-thick strips. In a large bowl, whisk the next
7 ingredients until blended. Pour 1 cup marinade into a shallow
dish. Add beef; turn to coat. Cover and refrigerate 2-8 hours.
Cover and refrigerate remaining marinade.

2. Preheat air fryer to 400°. Drain beef, discarding marinade in
dish. Thread beef onto 12 metal or soaked wooden skewers that
fit into air fryer. Working in batches if necessary, arrange
skewers in a single layer on greased tray in air-fryer basket.
Cook until meat reaches desired doneness (for medium-rare,
a thermometer should read 135°; medium, 140°; medium-well,
145°), 4-5 minutes, turning occasionally and basting frequently,
using ½ cup of reserved marinade.

3. Meanwhile, to make glaze, bring remaining marinade (about
¾ cup) to a boil; whisk in ½ tsp. cornstarch. Cook, whisking
constantly, until thickened, 1-2 minutes. Brush skewers with
glaze just before serving. If desired, top with sesame seeds
and sliced green onions.

2 KABOBS: 264 cal., 10g fat (4g sat. fat), 54mg chol., 1480mg sod.,
18g carb. (15g sugars, 0 fiber), 24g pro.

KITCHEN TIP: Using an air fryer saves space on the grill, but if
you don't own one or simply prefer a smoky grilled flavor, feel
free to toss these kabobs on the grill. Grill the kabobs, covered,
over medium-high heat until meat reaches desired doneness
(for medium-rare, a thermometer should read 135°; medium,
140°; medium-well, 145°), 4-5 minutes, turning occasionally and
basting frequently using ½ cup of reserved marinade.

GOLDEN PEACH PIE

2.

Years ago, I entered this pie in the Park County Fair in Livingston. It won a blue ribbon plus a purple ribbon for Best All Around. Family and friends agree with the judges—it's the perfect peach pie!

—Shirley Olson, Polson, MT

PREP: 20 MIN. • **BAKE:** 50 MIN. + COOLING • **MAKES:** 8 SERVINGS

2 **sheets refrigerated pie crust**
5 **cups sliced peeled fresh peaches (about 5 medium)**
2 **tsp. lemon juice**
½ **tsp. grated orange zest**
⅛ **tsp. almond extract**
1 **cup sugar**
¼ **cup cornstarch**
¼ **tsp. ground nutmeg**
⅛ **tsp. salt**
2 **Tbsp. butter**
   Optional: Heavy whipping cream and coarse sugar

1. Line a 9-in. pie plate with 1 sheet refrigerated crust; trim, leaving a 1-in. overhang around rim. Set aside. In a large bowl, combine the peaches, lemon juice, orange zest and extract. Combine the sugar, cornstarch, nutmeg and salt. Add to peach mixture; toss gently to coat. Pour into crust; dot with butter.

2. Roll out remaining crust to a ⅛-in.-thick circle; cut into strips. Arrange over filling in a lattice pattern. Trim and seal strips to bottom crust; fold overhang over. Lightly press or flute edge. If desired, brush lattice with heavy cream and sprinkle with sugar. Cover the edge loosely with foil.

3. Bake at 400° for 40 minutes. Remove foil; bake until crust is golden brown and filling is bubbly, 10-15 minutes longer. Cool on a wire rack. Store in the refrigerator.

1 PIECE: 425 cal., 17g fat (8g sat. fat), 18mg chol., 267mg sod., 67g carb. (36g sugars, 2g fiber), 3g pro.

A Day for Dad

Spiced Pulled Pork Sandwiches

Cleo's Potato Salad

Melon-Berry Salad

Buttery Horseradish
Corn on the Cob

Lemony Pineapple Iced Tea

Nutella Banana Cream Pie

SPICED PULLED PORK SANDWICHES

You'll love the fabulous spice rub on this tender pulled pork. It's my sweetie's favorite meal and a fantastic way to warm up on a chilly afternoon. Feel free to add more or less salt to taste.

—*Katie Citrowske, Bozeman, MT*

PREP: 30 MIN. • **COOK:** 6 HOURS • **MAKES:** 10 SERVINGS

1½ tsp. salt
1½ tsp. garlic powder
1½ tsp. ground cumin
1½ tsp. ground cinnamon
1½ tsp. chili powder
1½ tsp. coarsely ground pepper
1 boneless pork shoulder butt roast (3 to 4 lbs.), halved
2 Tbsp. olive oil
2 medium onions, halved and sliced
8 garlic cloves, coarsely chopped
1½ cups water
1 Tbsp. liquid smoke, optional
10 hamburger buns, split and toasted
Barbecue sauce
Sliced jalapeno pepper, optional

1. Mix seasonings; rub over pork. In a large skillet, heat oil over medium heat. Brown pork on all sides. Transfer to a 5- or 6-qt. slow cooker.

2. In same pan, cook and stir the onions over medium heat until lightly browned, 4-5 minutes. Add garlic; cook and stir 1 minute. Add water; bring to a boil, stirring to loosen browned bits from pan. If desired, stir in liquid smoke. Add to pork.

3. Cook, covered, on low until meat is tender, 6-8 hours. Remove roast; discard onion mixture. Shred pork with 2 forks; return to the slow cooker and heat through. Serve on buns with barbecue sauce and, if desired, jalapeno slices.

1 SANDWICH: 386 cal., 18g fat (6g sat. fat), 81mg chol., 669mg sod., 26g carb. (4g sugars, 2g fiber), 28g pro.

KITCHEN TIP: Pork shoulder butt roasts are the most common cut used for slow-cooked pulled pork sandwiches. If you can't find one in stores you can substitute a pork loin roast. This is a leaner cut of pork, though; it won't be as rich in flavor since it doesn't have as much fat as the shoulder.

CLEO'S POTATO SALAD

My mom, Cleo Lightfoot, loved cooking all kinds of different recipes, but her favorite meal was one she made when hosting backyard barbecues in the summer. She would make her famous ribs, baked beans and this delicious potato salad.

—*Joan Hallford, North Richland Hills, TX*

PREP: 25 MIN. • **COOK:** 20 MIN. • **MAKES:** 12 SERVINGS

3½ lbs. red potatoes
  (about 12 medium),
  cut into 1-in. cubes
6 bacon strips, chopped
¼ cup sugar
1 Tbsp. all-purpose flour
½ cup water
1 large egg, lightly beaten
3 Tbsp. cider vinegar
1 Tbsp. grated onion
1 tsp. celery seed
1 tsp. salt
½ tsp. pepper
1 cup heavy whipping
  cream, whipped
4 hard-boiled large
  eggs, chopped
2 medium celery
  ribs, chopped

1. Place potatoes in a large saucepan; cover with water. Bring to a boil. Reduce the heat; cook, uncovered, 10-15 minutes or until tender. Drain; cool completely.

2. Meanwhile, in a saucepan, cook the bacon over medium heat until crisp. Remove with a slotted spoon; drain on paper towels. Remove all but 1 Tbsp. drippings from pan.

3. Stir sugar and flour into drippings until smooth. Gradually stir in water; cook and stir over medium-high heat until thickened and bubbly. Remove from the heat. Stir a small amount of hot mixture into beaten egg; return all to pan, stirring constantly. Slowly bring to a boil, stirring constantly; remove from heat. Transfer to a large bowl; cool completely.

4. Gently stir in vinegar, onion and seasonings. Fold in whipped cream. Stir in eggs, celery, potatoes and bacon. Refrigerate, covered, until serving.

¾ CUP: 211 cal., 11g fat (5g sat. fat), 90mg chol., 272mg sod., 23g carb. (5g sugars, 2g fiber), 6g pro.

HAMMERSCHLAGEN

Hammerschlagen, a classic German game involving nails and hammers, is the perfect outdoor activity for a Father's Day celebration. Players take turns, using only one hand and the pointed end of a cross peen hammer, as they attempt to hit a designated nail flush with the surface of a tree stump or log.

MELON-BERRY SALAD

The best way to cool down on a warm day is with a chilled fruit salad. Serve this one for breakfast, brunch or dessert. Yogurt and coconut milk make the creamy dressing even more decadent.

—*Carrie Hirsch, Hilton Head Island, SC*

TAKES: 20 MIN. • **MAKES:** 12 SERVINGS

1 cup fat-free vanilla Greek yogurt
½ cup coconut milk
½ cup orange juice
4 cups cubed cantaloupe (½ in.)
4 cups cubed watermelon (½ in.)
2 medium navel oranges, sectioned
1 cup fresh raspberries
1 cup fresh blueberries
½ cup sweetened shredded coconut, toasted

1. For dressing, whisk together yogurt, coconut milk and orange juice. Refrigerate until serving.

2. To serve, place fruit in a large bowl; toss gently with dressing. Sprinkle with coconut.

NOTE: To toast coconut, bake in a shallow pan in a 350° oven for 5-10 minutes or cook in a skillet over low heat until golden brown, stirring occasionally.

¾ CUP: 105 cal., 3g fat (3g sat. fat), 0 chol., 30mg sod., 19g carb. (16g sugars, 2g fiber), 3g pro. **DIABETIC EXCHANGES:** 1 fruit, ½ fat.

KITCHEN TIP: The toasted coconut will get soggy if it sits on the fruit too long, so wait to garnish the salad until right before you're ready to serve.

BUTTERY HORSERADISH CORN ON THE COB

For a summer barbecue, I whipped up a butter and horseradish
topping for grilled corn. People actually formed a line to get seconds.

—Trish Loewen, Bakersfield, CA

TAKES: 30 MIN. • MAKES: 12 SERVINGS

¾ cup butter, softened
¼ cup shredded pepper
jack cheese
¼ cup prepared
horseradish
1 Tbsp. dried
parsley flakes
3 tsp. salt
2 tsp. balsamic vinegar
½ tsp. pepper
¼ tsp. dried thyme
12 medium ears sweet
corn, husked

1. In a small bowl, mix the first 8 ingredients until blended; spread over corn. Wrap each with a piece of heavy-duty foil (about 14 in. square), sealing tightly.

2. Grill corn, covered, over medium heat until tender, turning occasionally, 15-20 minutes. Open foil carefully to allow steam to escape.

1 EAR OF CORN: 203 cal., 14g fat (8g sat. fat), 33mg chol., 732mg sod., 20g carb. (7g sugars, 2g fiber), 4g pro.

LEMONY PINEAPPLE ICED TEA

I garnish this iced tea with some of our state's sweet Hawaiian pineapple. But you don't have to live on the islands to enjoy this fruity beverage—it's delicious everywhere!

—*Beverly Toomey, Honolulu, HI*

PREP: 20 MIN. + CHILLING • **COOK:** 10 MIN. • **MAKES:** 20 SERVINGS

16 cups water
24 tea bags
6 fresh mint sprigs
3⅓ cups sugar
3 cups unsweetened pineapple juice
1 cup lemon juice

1. In a stockpot, bring water to a boil; remove from the heat. Add tea bags; steep, covered, for 10 minutes. Discard tea bags. Add mint; steep 5 minutes. Discard mint. Add remaining ingredients, stirring to dissolve sugar.

2. Transfer to pitchers or a large covered container. Refrigerate, covered, until cold. If desired, serve with ice.

1 CUP: 154 cal., 0 fat (0 sat. fat), 0 chol., 7mg sod., 40g carb. (38g sugars, 0 fiber), 0 pro.

TREE-STUMP CHECKERS

The backyard becomes the setting of a test of skill and strategy with this clever DIY project.

MATERIALS
☐ Large tree stump
☐ Thick tree branch
☐ Black paint pen
☐ Black paint
☐ Paint in 2 colors
☐ Polycrylic finish
☐ Screw hook
☐ Muslin or canvas bag
☐ Orbital sander
☐ Paintbrush
☐ Miter saw

STEP 1
Using an orbital sander, sand the top of the tree stump.

STEP 2
Measure stump and calculate size of checkerboard, which should be 8 squares by 8 squares. Draw border and checkerboard spaces with paint pen, and fill in every other space with black paint. Dry thoroughly.

STEP 3
Apply polycrylic finish to seal top of stump. Dry thoroughly.

STEP 4
Using a miter saw, slice branch into 24 rounds, each ½ in. thick. Paint 12 checkers in one color and 12 in other color. Dry thoroughly.

STEP 5
Screw hook into side of stump. Store checkers in muslin bag and hang from hook.

NUTELLA BANANA CREAM PIE

Here's a banana cream pie with a little Italian flair. The chocolate and hazelnut go well with the banana, and the homemade pie crust makes it extra special. If you don't have time to melt and pipe the chocolate stars, just sprinkle the top of the pie with grated chocolate or cocoa powder.

—*Crystal Schlueter, Northglenn, CO*

PREP: 45 MIN. + CHILLING • **BAKE:** 20 MIN. + COOLING • **MAKES:** 10 SERVINGS

1¼ cups all-purpose flour
2 Tbsp. baking cocoa
1 Tbsp. sugar
½ cup cold butter, cubed
3 to 4 Tbsp. cold brewed coffee

DECORATIONS
¼ cup semisweet chocolate chips
¼ tsp. shortening

FILLING
1 carton (8 oz.) mascarpone cheese
¾ cup Nutella
2 medium bananas, thinly sliced
2 cups heavy whipping cream
3 Tbsp. instant banana cream pudding mix
2 Tbsp. chopped hazelnuts, toasted

1. In a small bowl, mix flour, cocoa and sugar; cut in butter until crumbly. Gradually add the cold coffee, tossing with a fork until dough holds together when pressed. Shape into a disk; wrap and refrigerate 1 hour or overnight.

2. On a lightly floured surface, roll dough to a ⅛-in.-thick circle; transfer to a 9-in. pie plate. Trim crust to ½ in. beyond rim of plate; flute edge. Refrigerate 30 minutes. Preheat oven to 425°.

3. Line crust with a double thickness of foil. Fill with pie weights, dried beans or uncooked rice. Bake on a lower oven rack until set, 15-20 minutes. Remove foil and weights; bake until edge is browned, about 5 minutes. Cool completely on a wire rack.

4. For decorations, in a microwave, melt chocolate chips and shortening; stir until smooth. Transfer to pastry bag with a small round tip. Pipe designs over a waxed paper-lined baking sheet. Freeze until set, about 5 minutes.

5. For filling, mix mascarpone cheese and Nutella until blended; spread into crust. Top with bananas.

6. In another bowl, beat cream until it begins to thicken. Add pudding mix; beat until stiff peaks form. Spread or pipe with a large star tip over bananas. Sprinkle with hazelnuts. Top with chocolate decorations.

NOTE: Let pie weights cool before storing. Beans and rice may be reused for pie weights, but not for cooking.

1 PIECE: 578 cal., 46g fat (24g sat. fat), 107mg chol., 147mg sod., 39g carb. (22g sugars, 2g fiber), 7g pro.

Red, White & Blue BBQ

Bratwurst & Chicken Kabobs

Americana
Frozen Lemonade

Feta Cheese-Stuffed Tomatoes

Gourmet Burgers with
Sun-Dried Tomato

Red, White & Blue Slaw

Red, White & Blue Dessert

BRATWURST & CHICKEN KABOBS

I made these lively kabobs as a thank-you gift while visiting my relatives
in Norway. They loved eating them almost as much as I loved cooking for them!
If you prefer less heat in the chutney, use honey in place of pepper jelly.
Also, any variety of vegetables will work for this recipe.

—Anna Davis, Springfield, MO

PREP: 40 MIN. • GRILL: 10 MIN. • MAKES: 12 KABOBS

¼ cup balsamic vinegar
¼ cup cider vinegar
2 Tbsp. pepper jelly
2 Tbsp. stone-ground
  mustard
1 tsp. salt
½ tsp. pepper
½ cup olive oil, divided
1 can (15 oz.) peach halves
  in light syrup, drained
  and cut into ½-in. cubes
⅔ cup minced onion
1 jar (12 oz.) mango chutney
6 boneless skinless
  chicken breasts
  (6 oz. each)
1 pkg. (14 oz.) fully cooked
  bratwurst links
2 each medium green
  pepper, sweet red pepper
  and yellow pepper
1 large onion
3 Tbsp. brown sugar
  bourbon seasoning

1. Whisk together vinegars, pepper jelly, mustard, salt and pepper. Gradually whisk in ⅓ cup olive oil until blended. Add peaches, minced onion and chutney. Set aside.

2. Cut chicken into 1-in. cubes and bratwursts into 1-in. slices. Cut peppers into large squares and onion into cubes. Toss with brown sugar bourbon seasoning and remaining oil.

3. On 12 metal or soaked wooden skewers, alternately thread meat and vegetables. Grill skewers, covered, on a greased grill rack over medium-high direct heat, turning occasionally, until chicken is no longer pink and vegetables are tender, 10-12 minutes. If desired, sprinkle with additional brown sugar bourbon seasoning during grilling. Serve with chutney.

NOTE: We used McCormick brown sugar bourbon seasoning for this recipe.

1 KABOB: 433 cal., 21g fat (5g sat. fat), 71mg chol., 1249mg sod., 37g carb. (24g sugars, 2g fiber), 23g pro.

AMERICANA FROZEN LEMONADE

This patriotic drink is as pretty as it is delicious. With cherries, blueberries and lemon juice, it has all the fresh summer flavors to quench your thirst.

—*Shawn Carleton, San Diego, CA*

TAKES: 10 MIN. • MAKES: 4 SERVINGS

1 cup lemon juice
1 cup sugar
4 cups ice cubes
1 cup fresh or frozen blueberries
  Maraschino cherries

Place lemon juice, sugar and ice in a blender; cover and process until slushy. Divide blueberries among 4 chilled glasses; muddle slightly. Add lemon slush; top with cherries.

¾ CUP: 229 cal., 0 fat (0 sat. fat), 0 chol., 1mg sod., 60g carb. (55g sugars, 1g fiber), 0 pro.

KITCHEN TIP: You may decide to opt for crushed ice instead of ice cubes when making this frozen drink. Crushed ice blends more easily and will give you that ideal thick, slushy consistency. Using larger cubes may damage your blender, but if that's all you have on hand, wrap the cubes in a clean towel and smash them with a rolling pin first.

FETA CHEESE-STUFFED TOMATOES

These tempting cheese-stuffed tomatoes are bursting with fresh
flavor. Use the small end of a melon scoop to easily remove the pulp.

—Laura LeRoy, Waxhaw, NC

TAKES: 25 MIN. • MAKES: 2 DOZEN

24 firm cherry tomatoes
3 oz. cream cheese,
   softened
⅓ cup crumbled feta cheese
¼ cup sour cream
1 green onion, finely
   chopped
¾ tsp. lemon juice
⅛ to ¼ tsp. dried oregano
   Coarsely ground pepper,
   optional

1. Cut a thin slice off the top of each tomato. Scoop out and discard pulp. Invert tomatoes onto paper towels to drain.

2. In a small mixing bowl, beat the cream cheese, feta cheese, sour cream, onion, lemon juice and oregano until blended. Pipe or spoon the cheese mixture into tomatoes. If desired, sprinkle with black pepper. Chill until serving.

1 STUFFED TOMATO: 25 cal., 2g fat (1g sat. fat), 6mg chol., 28mg sod., 1g carb. (1g sugars, 0 fiber), 1g pro.

KITCHEN TIP: To save time, prep the tomatoes and filling the night before your party, then fill the tomatoes before guests arrive the next day.

GOURMET BURGERS WITH SUN-DRIED TOMATO

This recipe brings together many of the flavors my family enjoys, complete
with a surprise in the center of each burger. You can use almost any cheese—
Gorgonzola, feta, smoked Gouda, blue or another favorite.

—Aaron Shields, Hamburg, NY

PREP: 40 MIN. • GRILL: 10 MIN. • MAKES: 8 SERVINGS

1 jar (7 oz.) oil-packed
  sun-dried tomatoes
3 medium onions, halved
  and thinly sliced
3 Tbsp. balsamic vinegar
½ cup finely chopped
  red onion
2 Tbsp. dried basil
2 tsp. ground cumin
2 tsp. ground
  chipotle pepper
½ tsp. salt
¼ tsp. pepper
3 lbs. lean ground
  beef (90% lean)
1 cup crumbled
  goat cheese
8 hamburger buns, split
  Mixed salad greens,
  optional

1. Drain the tomatoes, reserving ⅓ cup oil; set aside. In a large
skillet, saute sliced onions in 3 Tbsp. reserved oil until softened.
Add balsamic vinegar. Reduce the heat to medium-low; cook,
stirring occasionally, until deep golden brown, 30-40 minutes.

2. Meanwhile, chop sun-dried tomatoes and transfer to a large
bowl. Add the red onion, seasonings and remaining 7 tsp. of the
reserved oil. Crumble the beef over mixture and mix lightly but
thoroughly. Shape into 16 thin patties. Place 2 Tbsp. goat cheese
on the center of 8 patties. Top with remaining patties and press
edges firmly to seal.

3. Grill burgers, covered, over medium heat until a thermometer
reads 160° and juices run clear, 5-7 minutes on each side.

4. Place buns, cut side down, on grill until toasted, 1-2 minutes.
Serve burgers on buns with onions and, if desired, mixed salad
greens.

1 BURGER WITH 2 TBSP. ONIONS: 596 cal., 32g fat (10g sat. fat),
123mg chol., 588mg sod., 36g carb. (7g sugars, 5g fiber), 42g pro.

KITCHEN TIP: Use a gentle hand when shaping the burger patties.
Overworking the meat will make the cooked burgers less tender.

RED, WHITE & BLUE DESSERT

I altered a recipe I found and ended up with this rich and creamy berry trifle. Decorated to resemble a flag, it's perfect for the Fourth of July or any other patriotic occasion.

—Sue Gronholz, Beaver Dam, WI

TAKES: 20 MIN. • MAKES: 18 SERVINGS

2 pkg. (8 oz. each) cream cheese, softened
½ cup sugar
½ tsp. vanilla extract
½ tsp. almond extract
2 cups heavy whipping cream, whipped
2 qt. strawberries, halved, divided
2 qt. blueberries, divided

1. In a large bowl, beat the cream cheese, sugar and extracts until fluffy. Fold in whipped cream. Place a third of the cream mixture in a 4-qt. bowl. Reserve 20 strawberry halves and ½ cup blueberries for garnish.

2. Layer half of the remaining strawberries and blueberries over cream mixture. Top with another third of the cream mixture and the remaining berries. Spread the remaining cream mixture on top. Use the reserved strawberries and blueberries to make a flag on top.

1 CUP: 168 cal., 10g fat (6g sat. fat), 32mg chol., 44mg sod., 20g carb. (15g sugars, 3g fiber), 2g pro.

RED, WHITE & BLUE SLAW

This all-time favorite salad is perfect for any occasion, though obviously it's a great choice for a patriotic feast. You'll love the refreshing blend of ingredients.

—*Bonnie Hawkins, Elkhorn, WI*

TAKES: 10 MIN. • MAKES: 6 SERVINGS

6 cups angel hair
   coleslaw mix
12 cherry tomatoes, halved
¾ cup coleslaw
   salad dressing
¾ cup crumbled blue
   cheese, divided
½ cup real bacon bits

In a large bowl, combine the coleslaw mix, tomatoes, salad dressing and ½ cup blue cheese. Cover and refrigerate until serving. Just before serving, sprinkle with bacon bits and remaining cheese.

¾ CUP: 245 cal., 18g fat (5g sat. fat), 34mg chol., 960mg sod., 13g carb. (11g sugars, 2g fiber), 8g pro.

PATRIOTIC BANDANNA FLAG

Give the humble handkerchief a cheery new look with this colorful DIY flag.

MATERIALS

☐ Four 22-in.-sq. red bandannas

☐ Three 22-in.-sq.
   white bandannas

☐ One 22-in.-sq. blue bandanna

☐ Coordinating thread

☐ 26-in. dowel rod

☐ Twine

☐ 13 star-shaped lapel pins

☐ Scissors

☐ Sewing machine

☐ Straight pins

☐ Iron

STEP 1
Wash and dry bandannas.

STEP 2
Cut red and white bandannas into 5-in.-wide strips. Sew 2 red strips together at short end. Repeat with remaining red pieces for 7 long red strips. Repeat with white pieces for 6 long strips.

STEP 3
Fold 1½ in. of raw edge of each strip to back and press in place, leaving 2-in.-wide strip.

STEP 4
Fold 3 in. of each strip over the dowel rod and pin in place with the straight pins, alternating red and white stripes.

STEP 5
Fold blue bandanna to match width of 7 stripes (approximately 14 in.). Fold over dowel, covering left 7 stripes and adjusting to desired length. Secure with straight pins.

STEP 6
Cut 30 in. of twine and tie around ends of dowel to hang.

STEP 7
Once hanging, insert star-shaped pins at the top of each stripe to secure. Remove straight pins.

Fireworks Watching Party

Chocolate-Covered
Strawberry Snack Mix

Ultimate Club Roll-Ups

Summer Fresh Pasta Salad

Watermelon &
Blackberry Sangria

Dilly Chickpea Salad
Sandwiches

Chocolate Chip
Zucchini Cookies

Homemade Potato Chips

Roasted Strawberry
Sheet Cake

CHOCOLATE-COVERED STRAWBERRY SNACK MIX

I love indulging in chocolate-covered strawberries on special occasions. In fact, I love them so much I decided to experiment with a few ingredients to come up with an easy, everyday snack that captures the same flavors. Everyone is amazed when I pull this mix out at a picnic or tailgate, or on a road trip.

—TerryAnn Moore, Vineland, NJ

PREP: 15 MIN. + STANDING • **MAKES:** 10 SERVINGS (ABOUT 2 QT.)

6 cups Rice Chex
2 cups Chocolate Chex
1 cup semisweet chocolate chips
½ cup seedless strawberry jam
3 Tbsp. butter
1 tsp. almond extract
2 cups ground almonds
1 cup white baking chips
Sprinkles, optional

1. In a large bowl, combine the cereals. In a microwave, melt the chocolate chips, jam and butter; stir until smooth. Add the extract. Pour over cereal mixture and toss to coat. Sprinkle with almonds; toss to coat.

2. Immediately spread onto waxed paper. In a microwave, melt white chips; stir until smooth. Drizzle over cereal mixture. If desired, add sprinkles. Let stand until set. Break into pieces. Store in an airtight container.

¾ CUP: 443 cal., 24g fat (9g sat. fat), 11mg chol., 231mg sod., 55g carb. (33g sugars, 3g fiber), 7g pro.

FLASHY FAVORS

Your crew will have a blast with nonaerial fireworks before the big show. Place confetti poppers, snappers and sparklers in glass containers and let them have at it!

Set out some fun fireworks-watching swag, like snacks, glow sticks and earplugs. And don't forget the diffraction glasses! They make the display look totally out of this world.

ULTIMATE CLUB ROLL-UPS

Packed with deli meat, cheese and olives, these roll-ups will be the most-requested item in your picnic basket. Experiment with different ingredients and salad dressing flavors until you find the perfect combo.

—Linda Searl, Pampa, TX

TAKES: 25 MIN. • MAKES: 8 SERVINGS

3 oz. cream cheese, softened
½ cup ranch salad dressing
2 Tbsp. ranch salad dressing mix
8 bacon strips, cooked and crumbled
½ cup finely chopped onion
1 can (2¼ oz.) sliced ripe olives, drained
1 jar (2 oz.) diced pimientos, drained
¼ cup diced canned jalapeno peppers
8 flour tortillas (10 in.), room temperature
8 thin slices deli ham
8 thin slices deli turkey
8 thin slices deli roast beef
2 cups shredded cheddar cheese

1. In a small bowl, beat the cream cheese, ranch dressing and dressing mix until well blended. In another bowl, combine the bacon, onion, olives, pimientos and jalapenos.

2. Spread cream cheese mixture over tortillas; layer with ham, turkey and roast beef. Sprinkle with bacon mixture and cheddar cheese; roll up.

1 ROLL-UP: 554 cal., 29g fat (12g sat. fat), 80mg chol., 1802mg sod., 39g carb. (2g sugars, 7g fiber), 27g pro.

KITCHEN TIP: Hosting a large crowd on the Fourth of July? You can also cut these roll-ups into thirds and secure each section with a toothpick to serve as a cold appetizer.

SUMMER FRESH PASTA SALAD

We love this fast and easy pasta salad that's loaded with seasonal fresh fruits and veggies. I serve it with almond crackers and slices of sharp cheddar cheese.
—*Cathy Orban, Chandler, AZ*

PREP: 20 MIN. + CHILLING • **MAKES:** 12 SERVINGS

4 cups uncooked campanelle or spiral pasta
2 medium carrots, finely chopped
2 medium peaches, chopped
1 pouch (11 oz.) light tuna in water
½ cup sliced celery
½ cup julienned cucumber
½ cup julienned zucchini
½ cup fresh broccoli florets, chopped
½ cup grated red cabbage
½ tsp. salt
½ tsp. pepper
2 cups Caesar salad dressing

Cook pasta according to package directions for al dente. Drain; rinse with cold water and drain well. Transfer to a large bowl. Add carrots, peaches, tuna, celery, cucumber, zucchini, broccoli, cabbage, salt and pepper. Drizzle with dressing; toss to coat. Refrigerate, covered, at least 3 hours before serving.

¾ CUP: 357 cal., 23g fat (4g sat. fat), 25mg chol., 651mg sod., 26g carb. (5g sugars, 2g fiber), 10g pro.

SERVE IT WITH:
Spiced Pulled Pork Sandwiches, Page 117

UTENSIL HOLDER
A convenient carrier corrals napkins and utensils when you're on the go. Pop in a mini flag for some extra fun!

WATERMELON & BLACKBERRY SANGRIA

This recipe is deliciously pink! Living in the zinfandel wine country of Northern California's Gold Country, I use our local fare in my recipes. I garnish it with sprigs of mint or basil for personal flair. This easy recipe is perfect for entertaining, and it's especially brunch friendly.

—*Carolyn Kumpe, El Dorado, CA*

PREP: 5 MIN. + CHILLING • **MAKES:** 8 SERVINGS

1 bottle (750 ml) white zinfandel or rose wine, chilled
¼ cup watermelon schnapps liqueur
1½ cups cubed seedless watermelon (½-in. cubes)
1 medium lime, thinly sliced
½ to 1 cup fresh blackberries, halved
1 can (12 oz.) lemon-lime soda, chilled
Ice cubes
Fresh basil or mint leaves

In a large pitcher, stir together the wine and schnapps; add the watermelon, lime and blackberries. Chill at least 2 hours. Just before serving, stir in soda. Serve over ice. Garnish with basil or mint.

¾ CUP: 119 cal., 0 fat (0 sat. fat), 0 chol., 10mg sod., 12g carb. (8g sugars, 1g fiber), 0 pro.

PEACH & RASPBERRY SANGRIA: Substitute peach schnapps or raspberry liquor for the melon liquor, and use fresh peaches and raspberries instead of the watermelon and blackberries.

DILLY CHICKPEA SALAD SANDWICHES

This chickpea salad is super flavorful and contains less fat and cholesterol than chicken salad. These make delightful picnic sandwiches.

—Deanna Wolfe, Muskegon, MI

TAKES: 15 MIN. • MAKES: 6 SERVINGS

1 can (15 oz.) chickpeas or garbanzo beans, rinsed and drained
½ cup finely chopped onion
½ cup finely chopped celery
½ cup reduced-fat mayonnaise or vegan mayonnaise
3 Tbsp. honey mustard or Dijon mustard
2 Tbsp. snipped fresh dill
1 Tbsp. red wine vinegar
¼ tsp. salt
¼ tsp. paprika
¼ tsp. pepper
12 slices multigrain bread
Optional: Romaine leaves, tomato slices, dill pickle slices and sweet red pepper rings

Place chickpeas in a large bowl; mash to desired consistency. Stir in onion, celery, mayonnaise, mustard, dill, vinegar, salt, paprika and pepper. Spread over each of 6 bread slices; layer with toppings of your choice and remaining bread.

1 SANDWICH: 295 cal., 11g fat (2g sat. fat), 7mg chol., 586mg sod., 41g carb. (9g sugars, 7g fiber), 10g pro.

KITCHEN TIP: Chickpeas, also commonly called garbanzo beans, are medium-sized tan and acorn-shaped beans. They are packed with many vitamins and nutrients in addition to being high in fiber and protein. They make a great meat substitute for those who follow a plant-based diet.

CHOCOLATE CHIP ZUCCHINI COOKIES

I love incorporating garden-fresh zucchini into baked goods, especially these cookies that are perfect for family reunions and summer potlucks. These treats are similar in flavor to a zucchini quick bread my aunt makes. The cookies taste better if you make them the day before.

—*Melissa Obernesser, Oriskany, NY*

PREP: 15 MIN. • **BAKE:** 12 MIN./BATCH • **MAKES:** 4 DOZEN

½ cup unsalted
   butter, softened
½ cup sugar
⅓ cup packed brown sugar
1 large egg, room
   temperature
1½ tsp. vanilla extract
1 cup all-purpose flour
½ cup whole wheat flour
1 tsp. ground cinnamon
½ tsp. baking soda
¼ tsp. salt
1½ cups shredded zucchini
1 cup quick-cooking oats
1 cup semisweet
   chocolate chips
¾ cup chopped
   pecans, toasted

1. Preheat oven to 350°. In a large bowl, cream the butter and sugars until light and fluffy, 5-7 minutes. Beat in egg and vanilla. In another bowl, whisk flours, cinnamon, baking soda and salt; gradually beat into the creamed mixture. Stir in the remaining ingredients.

2. Drop dough by tablespoonfuls 2 in. apart onto greased baking sheets. Bake until edges start to brown, 12-14 minutes. Cool on pans for 2 minutes. Remove to wire racks to cool. Store between pieces of waxed paper in an airtight container.

1 COOKIE: 79 cal., 4g fat (2g sat. fat), 9mg chol., 27mg sod., 10g carb. (6g sugars, 1g fiber), 1g pro.

HOMEMADE POTATO CHIPS

What's a picnic basket without everyone's favorite salty snack tucked inside?
Skip overpriced store-bought bags of potato chips and make these at home instead.
—Taste of Home *Test Kitchen*

PREP: 30 MIN. + SOAKING • **COOK:** 5 MIN./BATCH • **MAKES:** 11 SERVINGS (8½ CUPS)

7 unpeeled medium
   potatoes (about 2 lbs.)
2 qt. ice water
5 tsp. salt
2 tsp. garlic powder
1½ tsp. celery salt
1½ tsp. pepper
   Oil for deep-fat frying

1. Using a vegetable peeler, cut potatoes into very thin slices. Place in a bowl; add ice water and salt. Soak for 30 minutes.

2. Drain potatoes; place on paper towels and pat dry. In a bowl, combine the garlic powder, celery salt and pepper; set aside.

3. In a cast-iron skillet, heat 1½ in. oil to 375°. Fry potatoes in batches until golden brown, 3-4 minutes, stirring frequently.

4. Remove potatoes with a slotted spoon; drain on paper towels. Immediately sprinkle with seasoning mixture. Store chips in an airtight container.

¾ CUP: 176 cal., 8g fat (1g sat. fat), 0 chol., 703mg sod., 24g carb. (1g sugars, 3g fiber), 3g pro.

PATRIOTIC PICNIC BOWL COVERS

Keep your food safe from bugs, rain and wind-blown debris with these handmade bowl covers.

MATERIALS

☐ 3 cotton bandannas

☐ Iron-on vinyl sheet

☐ 3 yd. extra-wide double-fold bias tape in coordinating color

☐ 9 ft. 3mm elastic cord

☐ Scissors

☐ Iron

☐ Straight pins

☐ Large blunt needle

STEP 1
Wash and dry bandannas.

STEP 2
Cut a circle from each bandanna to a diameter that will fit desired bowls—standard sizes are 11, 13 and 15 in.

STEP 3
Cut a coordinating piece of iron-on vinyl for each circle. Apply it to one side of each circle according to manufacturer's instructions.

STEP 4
Fold bias tape around outer edge of circle, overlapping ends 1 in. Pin in place. Topstitch bias tape around the circle, leaving a 1½ in. opening to insert elastic.

STEP 5
Cut a length of elastic 2 in. longer than the circumference of the circle. Insert elastic through bias tape using blunt needle, carefully working elastic around the circle. Cinch elastic to fit bowl and tie ends together in a secure square knot. Stitch opening closed.

STEP 6
Repeat the process with the remaining 2 bandanna circles.

STEP 7
To clean bowl covers, wipe with a damp cloth or hand-wash in cold water and hang to dry.

ROASTED STRAWBERRY SHEET CAKE

My Grandma Gigi loved summer berry cakes. Almost any time I'd call her during the warmer months, she'd invite me over to taste her latest masterpiece. This cake is an ode to her.

—Kristin Bowers, Rancho Palos Verdes, CA

PREP: 1 HOUR • **BAKE:** 30 MIN. + COOLING • **MAKES:** 24 SERVINGS

4 lbs. halved fresh strawberries
½ cup sugar

CAKE
1 cup butter, softened
1½ cups sugar
2 large eggs, room temperature
2 tsp. almond extract
3 cups all-purpose flour
3 tsp. baking powder
2 tsp. salt
1 cup 2% milk
¼ cup turbinado (washed raw) sugar

1. Preheat oven to 350°. Place strawberries on a parchment-lined rimmed baking sheet. Sprinkle with sugar and toss to coat. Bake until just tender, 35-40 minutes. Cool slightly.

2. Meanwhile, grease a 15x10x1-in. baking pan. In a large bowl, cream butter and sugar until light and fluffy, 5-7 minutes. Add eggs, 1 at a time, beating well after each addition. Beat in the extract. In another bowl, whisk flour, baking powder and salt; add to creamed mixture alternately with milk, beating well after each addition (batter may appear curdled).

3. Transfer cake batter to prepared pan. Top with 3 cups roasted strawberries; sprinkle with turbinado sugar. Reserve remaining strawberries for serving. Bake until a toothpick inserted in the center comes out clean, 30-35 minutes. Cool completely in pan on a wire rack. Serve with reserved roasted strawberries.

1 PIECE: 235 cal., 9g fat (5g sat. fat), 37mg chol., 329mg sod., 37g carb. (23g sugars, 2g fiber), 3g pro.

AUTUMN
GET-TOGETHERS

Hearty Farmhouse Breakfast

Sour Cream Swiss Steak

Campfire Scrambled Eggs

Sausage Hash

Cold-Brew Coffee

Slow-Cooker Coconut Granola

Cowboy Cornbread

Chocolate Walnut Ring

Pecan Coffee Cake

SOUR CREAM SWISS STEAK

I spent a year searching for new and different beef recipes. This is the dish that my family raves about, and they agree that it's a nice change from regular Swiss steak.

—*Barb Benting, Grand Rapids, MI*

PREP: 50 MIN. • BAKE: 1½ HOURS • MAKES: 8 SERVINGS

⅓ cup plus 3 Tbsp.
all-purpose flour, divided
1½ tsp. each salt,
pepper, paprika and
ground mustard
3 lbs. beef top round
steak, cut into
serving-size pieces
3 Tbsp. canola oil
3 Tbsp. butter
1½ cups water
1½ cups sour cream
1 cup finely chopped onion
2 garlic cloves, minced
⅓ cup soy sauce
¼ to ⅓ cup packed
brown sugar
Additional paprika,
optional

1. In a shallow bowl, combine ⅓ cup flour, salt, pepper, paprika and ground mustard; dredge the steak.

2. In a large skillet, heat the oil and butter. Cook steak on both sides until browned. Carefully add water; cover and simmer for 30 minutes.

3. In a bowl, combine sour cream, onion, garlic, soy sauce, brown sugar and the remaining flour; stir until smooth. Transfer steak to a greased 2½-qt. baking dish; add sour cream mixture.

4. Cover and bake at 325° for 1½ hours or until tender. Sprinkle with paprika if desired.

1 SERVING: 460 cal., 23g fat (10g sat. fat), 137mg chol., 1173mg sod., 17g carb. (10g sugars, 1g fiber), 43g pro.

CAMPFIRE SCRAMBLED EGGS

Every bit as quick as scrambled eggs are meant to be, this hearty dish— with
red pimientos and green parsley or chives— is nice for hectic mornings.

—Fern Raleigh, Windom, KS

TAKES: 20 MIN. • MAKES: 6 SERVINGS

12 large eggs
1½ cups 2% milk, divided
½ to 1 tsp. salt
¼ tsp. pepper
2 Tbsp. diced pimientos
2 Tbsp. minced fresh
   parsley or chives
2 Tbsp. all-purpose flour
¼ cup butter, cubed

In a large bowl, beat eggs and 1 cup milk. Add salt, pepper, pimientos and parsley. In a small bowl, combine flour and remaining milk until smooth; stir into the egg mixture. In a large cast-iron or other heavy skillet, melt the butter over medium heat. Add egg mixture. Cook and stir over medium heat until the eggs are completely set.

1 SERVING: 185 cal., 11g fat (4g sat. fat), 377mg chol., 369mg sod., 6g carb. (3g sugars, 0 fiber), 15g pro.

SAUSAGE HASH

We always have plenty of pork sausage around, so when I need a quick meal, I use
this handy recipe. The colorful vegetables give the hash a bold look to match its flavor.

—Virginia Krites, Cridersville, OH

PREP: 10 MIN. • COOK: 30 MIN. • MAKES: 6 SERVINGS

1 lb. bulk pork sausage
1 medium onion, chopped
2 medium carrots, grated
1 medium green
  pepper, chopped
3 cups diced cooked
  potatoes
½ tsp. salt
¼ tsp. pepper

In a large cast-iron or other heavy skillet, cook sausage over medium heat until no longer pink; drain. Add the onion, carrots and green pepper; cook until tender. Stir in potatoes, salt and pepper. Reduce heat; cook and stir until lightly browned and heated through, about 20 minutes.

1 CUP: 245 cal., 14g fat (5g sat. fat), 27mg chol., 519mg sod., 22g carb. (5g sugars, 3g fiber), 8g pro.

COLD-BREW COFFEE

Cold brewing reduces the acidity of coffee, which enhances its natural sweetness and complex flavors. Even those who take hot coffee with sugar and cream might find themselves sipping cold brew plain.

—Taste of Home *Test Kitchen*

PREP: 10 MIN. + CHILLING • **MAKES:** 8 SERVINGS

1 cup coarsely ground medium-roast coffee
1 cup hot water (205°)
6 to 7 cups cold water
Optional: 2% milk or half-and-half cream

1. Place the coffee grounds in a clean glass container. Pour hot water over the grounds; let stand 10 minutes. Stir in cold water. Cover and refrigerate for 12-24 hours. (The longer the coffee sits, the stronger the flavor.)

2. Strain the coffee through a fine mesh sieve; discard grounds. Strain the coffee again through a coffee filter; discard grounds. Serve over ice, with milk or cream if desired. Store coffee in the refrigerator for up to 2 weeks.

1 CUP: 2 cal., 0 fat (0 sat. fat), 0 chol., 4mg sod., 0 carb. (0 sugars, 0 fiber), 0 pro.

KITCHEN TIP: Some people enjoy a tiny pinch of salt instead of sugar in cold brews. Salt brings out the inherent sweetness of the coffee.

CHOCOLATE WALNUT RING

This is an adaptation of my wife's recipe. It's terrific for a special
brunch or even as a midmorning snack.

—Peter Halferty, Corpus Christi, TX

PREP: 55 MIN. + RISING • **BAKE:** 20 MIN. + COOLING • **MAKES:** 20 SERVINGS

3 to 3½ cups
   all-purpose flour
¼ cup sugar
1 pkg. (¼ oz.) active
   dry yeast
1 tsp. ground cinnamon
½ tsp. salt
½ cup 2% milk
¼ cup water
2 Tbsp. butter
2 Tbsp. canola oil
1 large egg, room
   temperature
1 large egg yolk, room
   temperature

FILLING
½ cup miniature semisweet
   chocolate chips
½ cup chopped walnuts
3 Tbsp. brown sugar

GLAZE
⅔ cup confectioners' sugar
⅛ tsp. ground cinnamon
¼ tsp. vanilla extract
3 to 4 tsp. whole milk

1. In a large bowl, combine 1 cup flour, sugar, yeast, cinnamon and salt. In a small saucepan, heat milk, water, butter and oil to 120°-130°. Add to dry ingredients; beat just until moistened. Add egg and yolk; beat until smooth. Stir in enough remaining flour to form a soft dough (dough will be sticky).

2. Turn onto a floured surface; knead until smooth and elastic, 6-8 minutes. Place in a greased bowl, turning once to grease top. Cover and let rise in a warm place until doubled, about 1 hour. Combine filling ingredients in a small bowl; set aside.

3. Punch dough down. Turn onto a lightly floured surface. Roll into an 18x9-in. rectangle; sprinkle with filling to within 1 in. of edges. Roll up tightly jelly-roll style, starting with a long side; seal ends.

4. Place seam side down on a greased baking sheet; pinch ends together to form a ring. With scissors, cut from outside edge two-thirds of the way toward the center of the ring at 1-in. intervals. Separate strips slightly; twist to allow the filling to show. Cover and let rise until doubled, about 40 minutes.

5. Preheat oven to 350°. Bake 18-22 minutes or until golden brown. Remove to a wire rack to cool completely. Combine glaze ingredients; drizzle over ring.

1 PIECE: 175 cal., 7g fat (2g sat. fat), 25mg chol., 79mg sod., 27g carb. (11g sugars, 1g fiber), 4g pro.

PECAN COFFEE CAKE

My mom serves this nutty coffee cake for Christmas breakfast each year. The simple recipe is a big timesaver on such an event-filled morning. Everyone loves the crunchy topping.
—*Becky Wax, Tuscola, IL*

PREP: 15 MIN. • **BAKE:** 30 MIN. • **MAKES:** 15 SERVINGS

1 pkg. yellow cake
  mix (regular size)
1 pkg. (3.4 oz.) instant
  vanilla pudding mix
1 cup sour cream
4 large eggs, room
  temperature
⅓ cup canola oil
2 tsp. vanilla extract
⅔ cup chopped pecans
⅓ cup sugar
2 tsp. ground cinnamon
½ cup confectioners' sugar
2 Tbsp. orange juice

1. In a large bowl, beat the first 6 ingredients on low speed for 30 seconds. Beat on medium for 2 minutes. Pour into a greased 13x9-in. baking pan. Combine pecans, sugar and cinnamon; sprinkle over batter. Cut through the batter with a knife to swirl pecan mixture.

2. Bake at 350° for 30-35 minutes or until a toothpick inserted in the center comes out clean.

3. Meanwhile, in a small bowl, combine confectioners' sugar and orange juice until smooth; drizzle over warm coffee cake. Cool on a wire rack.

1 PIECE: 335 cal., 16g fat (4g sat. fat), 67mg chol., 332mg sod., 44g carb. (29g sugars, 1g fiber), 4g pro.

SLOW-COOKER COCONUT GRANOLA

Here's a versatile treat with a taste of the tropics. Mix it up by
subbing dried pineapple or tropical fruits for the cherries.
—Taste of Home *Test Kitchen*

PREP: 15 MIN. • **COOK:** 3½ HOURS • **MAKES:** 12 SERVINGS

4 **cups old-fashioned oats**
1 **cup sliced almonds**
1 **cup unsweetened
   coconut flakes**
1 **tsp. ground cinnamon**
1 **tsp. ground ginger**
¼ **tsp. salt**
½ **cup coconut oil, melted**
½ **cup maple syrup**
1 **cup dried cherries**

1. Combine oats, almonds, coconut, cinnamon, ginger and salt in
a 3-qt. slow cooker. In small bowl, whisk together oil and maple
syrup. Pour into slow cooker; stir to combine. Cook, covered, on
low, stirring occasionally, 3½-4 hours. Stir in cherries.

2. Transfer mixture to a baking sheet; let stand until cool.

½ CUP: 343 cal., 19g fat (12g sat. fat), 0 chol., 55mg sod., 41g carb.
(18g sugars, 5g fiber), 6g pro.

KITCHEN TIP: Pack this granola in small containers or resealable
storage bags for a portable snack throughout the workweek.

COWBOY CORNBREAD

This cornbread is richer and sweeter than others I've tried.
It's especially luscious alongside ham and beans.

—Karen Ann Bland, Gove, KS

PREP: 15 MIN. • **BAKE:** 25 MIN. • **MAKES:** 12 SERVINGS

2 cups biscuit/baking mix
1 cup yellow cornmeal
¾ cup sugar
½ tsp. baking soda
½ tsp. salt
2 large eggs, room
temperature
1 cup butter, melted
1 cup half-and-half cream

SERVE IT WITH:
Homemade Apple Cider
Beef Stew, Page 178

1. In a large bowl, combine first 5 ingredients. In another bowl, combine the eggs, butter and cream; stir into dry ingredients just until moistened. Spread into a greased 13x9-in. baking pan.

2. Bake at 350° until a toothpick inserted in the center comes out clean, 25-30 minutes. Serve warm.

1 PIECE: 345 cal., 21g fat (12g sat. fat), 85mg chol., 532mg sod., 34g carb. (14g sugars, 1g fiber), 4g pro.

Homemade Harvest Fest

Citrus Cider Punch

Sweet Potato & Chorizo
Croquettes

Potato Pan Rolls

Pumpkin Black Bean Soup

Homemade Apple Cider
Beef Stew

Spiced Sweet Potato
Doughnuts

Caramel Apples

Autumn Harvest
Pumpkin Pie

CITRUS CIDER PUNCH

I share this refreshing punch recipe with people who visit our apple cider mill. It's the perfect beverage for autumn gatherings.
—*Carolyn Beck, St Johns, MI*

TAKES: 5 MIN. • MAKES: 19 SERVINGS (4¾ QT.)

1 gallon apple cider, chilled
1 can (12 oz.) frozen lemonade concentrate, thawed
1 medium lemon, sliced
4 spiced apple rings

In a large punch bowl, combine cider and lemonade. Add lemon slices and apple rings. If desired, serve with additional lemon slices and apple rings.

1 CUP: 138 cal., 0 fat (0 sat. fat), 0 chol., 22mg sod., 35g carb. (30g sugars, 0 fiber), 0 pro.

SWEET POTATO & CHORIZO CROQUETTES

Chorizo and paprika add smokiness to these crispy bites. For a harvest party, make them into little pumpkins using pretzel sticks and cilantro leaves.
—*Nick Iverson, Denver, CO*

PREP: 55 MIN. + CHILLING • COOK: 5 MIN./BATCH • MAKES: 3 DOZEN

2 large sweet potatoes (about 12 oz. each), cut into 1-in. pieces
1 Tbsp. canola oil
14 oz. fresh chorizo or bulk spicy pork sausage
2 cups (8 oz.) queso fresco or shredded Mexican cheese blend
1 large egg
½ tsp. smoked paprika
¼ tsp. salt
¼ tsp. pepper
¾ cup panko bread crumbs
  Oil for deep-fat frying
  Pretzel sticks and fresh cilantro leaves

1. Preheat oven to 400° Place sweet potatoes on a 15x10x1-in. baking pan. Drizzle with oil; toss to coat. Roast the potatoes 30-40 minutes or until tender. Meanwhile, in a large skillet, cook chorizo over medium heat 6-8 minutes or until no longer pink. Drain and transfer to a large bowl.

2. Mash potatoes; add to chorizo. Stir in cheese, egg, paprika, salt and pepper. Refrigerate until cold, about 1 hour.

3. Shape into 1¼-in. balls. Place bread crumbs in a shallow bowl. Roll balls in crumbs to coat. In an electric skillet or a deep fryer, heat oil to 375°. Fry balls in batches 4-6 minutes or until golden brown, turning occasionally. Drain on paper towels.

4. Decorate with pretzel sticks and cilantro.

1 CROQUETTE: 110 cal., 8g fat (2g sat. fat), 19mg chol., 174mg sod., 6g carb. (2g sugars, 1g fiber), 5g pro.

POTATO PAN ROLLS

My family loves these rolls and requests them often. They don't take long to make because you use quick-rise yeast.
—*Connie Storckman, Evanston, WY*

PREP: 15 MIN. + RISING • **BAKE:** 20 MIN. • **MAKES:** 16 ROLLS

4½ to 5 cups all-purpose flour
3 Tbsp. sugar
2 pkg. (¼ oz. each) quick-rise yeast
1½ tsp. salt
1¼ cups water
3 Tbsp. butter
½ cup mashed potatoes (without added milk and butter)
Additional all-purpose flour

1. In a large bowl, combine 2 cups flour, sugar, yeast and salt. In a small saucepan, heat water and butter to 120°-130°. Add to dry ingredients; beat until smooth. Stir in mashed potatoes and enough remaining flour to form a soft dough.

2. Turn onto a floured surface; knead until smooth and elastic, 6-8 minutes. Cover and let rest for 10 minutes. Divide into 16 pieces. Shape each into a ball. Place in two greased 8- or 9-in. cast-iron skillets or round baking pans. Cover and let rise in a warm place until doubled, about 30 minutes.

3. Preheat oven to 400°. Sprinkle tops of rolls with additional flour. Bake until golden brown, 18-22 minutes. Remove from pans to wire racks.

1 ROLL: 163 cal., 3g fat (1g sat. fat), 6mg chol., 239mg sod., 30g carb. (3g sugars, 1g fiber), 4g pro.

KITCHEN TIP: The mashed potatoes in these rolls help them stay soft longer than other rolls that turn stale in a day or two. Wrapped tightly and stored at room temperature, Potato Pan Rolls can keep up to 7 days.

PUMPKIN BLACK BEAN SOUP

I picked up this recipe at my local grocery store during a promotion for creative ways to use pumpkin. Black beans are not usually paired with this hearty fall vegetable, but once I tried this soup, I was a believer! Now it's one of my favorite recipes to make when pumpkin is in season.

—*Lori Karavolis, McMurray, PA*

PREP: 30 MIN. • COOK: 20 MIN. • MAKES: 10 SERVINGS (2½ QT)

2 Tbsp. olive oil
1 cup chopped sweet onion
1 garlic clove, minced
½ cup white wine
2 cans (15 oz. each) black beans, rinsed and drained
1 can (28 oz.) diced tomatoes, undrained
2 cups vegetable broth
1 can (15 oz.) pumpkin
4 tsp. ground coriander
3 tsp. ground cumin
¾ tsp. salt
¼ tsp. cayenne pepper
¼ tsp. pepper
1 cup heavy whipping cream
   Optional: Chopped fresh cilantro and tortilla chips

1. In a Dutch oven, heat oil over medium-high heat. Add onion; cook and stir until tender, 4-5 minutes. Add the garlic; cook 1 minute longer. Stir in wine. Bring to a boil; cook until liquid is reduced by half, 3-4 minutes.

2. Add black beans, tomatoes, broth, pumpkin and seasonings. Bring to a boil; reduce heat. Simmer, covered, until the flavors are blended, about 20 minutes, stirring occasionally. Add cream; heat through. If desired, top with chopped cilantro and tortilla chips.

FREEZE OPTION: Freeze cooled soup in freezer containers. To use, partially thaw in refrigerator overnight. Heat through, stirring occasionally; add broth if necessary.

1 CUP: 221 cal., 12g fat (6g sat. fat), 27mg chol., 608mg sod., 23g carb. (6g sugars, 7g fiber), 6g pro.

HOMEMADE APPLE CIDER BEEF STEW

We start craving this comforting stew as soon as weather gets cold and Nebraska's apple orchards start selling fresh cider. Its subtle sweetness is a welcome change from other savory stews. We enjoy it with biscuits, sliced apples and cheddar cheese.

—*Joyce Glaesemann, Lincoln, NE*

PREP: 30 MIN. • **COOK:** 1¾ HOURS • **MAKES:** 8 SERVINGS

2 lbs. beef stew meat, cut into 1-in. cubes
2 Tbsp. canola oil
3 cups apple cider or juice
1 can (14½ oz.) reduced-sodium beef broth
2 Tbsp. cider vinegar
1½ tsp. salt
¼ to ½ tsp. dried thyme
¼ tsp. pepper
3 medium potatoes, peeled and cubed
4 medium carrots, cut into ¾-in. pieces
3 celery ribs, cut into ¾-in. pieces
2 medium onions, cut into wedges
¼ cup all-purpose flour
¼ cup water
Fresh thyme sprigs, optional

1. In a Dutch oven, brown beef on all sides in oil over medium-high heat; drain. Add the cider, broth, vinegar, salt, thyme and pepper; bring to a boil. Reduce heat; cover and simmer for 1¼ hours.

2. Add the potatoes, carrots, celery and onions; return to a boil. Reduce heat; cover and simmer for 30-35 minutes or until beef and vegetables are tender.

3. Combine flour and water until smooth; stir into stew. Bring to a boil; cook and stir for 2 minutes or until thickened. If desired, serve with fresh thyme.

1 CUP: 330 cal., 12g fat (3g sat. fat), 72mg chol., 628mg sod., 31g carb. (14g sugars, 2g fiber), 24g pro. **DIABETIC EXCHANGES:** 3 lean meat, 1½ starch, 1 vegetable.

SPICED SWEET POTATO DOUGHNUTS

This sweet potato dessert (or decadent breakfast) is easy to prepare.
And no one minds eating the nutritious spuds when they're inside doughnuts!

—*Jan Valdez, Lombard, IL*

PREP: 15 MIN. • **COOK:** 5 MIN./BATCH • **MAKES:** 1 DOZEN

3 Tbsp. butter, softened
1 cup sugar
3 large eggs, room
  temperature
1 cup mashed sweet
  potatoes
½ cup buttermilk
1 tsp. vanilla extract
3½ cups self-rising flour
2 Tbsp. pumpkin pie spice
¾ tsp. salt
  Oil for deep-fat frying

TOPPING
1 cup sugar
4 tsp. ground cinnamon

1. In a large bowl, beat the butter and sugar until blended. Beat in the eggs, sweet potatoes, buttermilk and vanilla. In another bowl, whisk flour, pumpkin pie spice and salt; gradually beat into creamed mixture.

2. Turn onto a well-floured surface; pat to ½-in. thickness. Cut with a floured 3-in. doughnut cutter. In an electric skillet or deep fryer, heat oil to 375°. Fry doughnuts, a few at a time, until golden brown, 2-3 minutes on each side. Drain on paper towels. In a small bowl, mix sugar and cinnamon; dip warm doughnuts in topping mixture to coat both sides.

1 DOUGHNUT: 383 cal., 14g fat (3g sat. fat), 55mg chol., 651mg sod., 59g carb. (27g sugars, 2g fiber), 6g pro.

SHAPING DOUGHNUTS

All you need to flatten this dough is your hands. Pat it down, then cut with a doughnut cutter. To keep the dough from sticking, dip your cutter in a little flour between cuts.

CARAMEL APPLES

Who doesn't love a good, gooey caramel apple? Make a double batch because these treats always go fast!
—*Karen Ann Bland, Gove, KS*

PREP: 10 MIN. • **COOK:** 30 MIN. • **MAKES:** 16 SERVINGS (8 APPLES)

1 **cup butter**
2 **cups packed brown sugar**
1 **cup light corn syrup**
1 **can (14 oz.) sweetened condensed milk**
1 **tsp. vanilla extract**
8 **wooden sticks**
8 **medium tart apples**
  Unsalted peanuts, chopped, optional

In a heavy 3-qt. saucepan, combine butter, brown sugar, corn syrup and milk; bring to a boil over medium-high heat. Cook and stir until mixture reaches 248° (firm-ball stage) on a candy thermometer, 30-40 minutes. Remove from the heat; stir in vanilla. Insert wooden sticks into apples. Dip each apple into hot caramel mixture; turn to coat. Set on waxed paper to cool. If desired, gently roll the bottom of the dipped apples into chopped peanuts.

½ APPLE: 388 cal., 14g fat (9g sat. fat), 39mg chol., 145mg sod., 68g carb. (65g sugars, 2g fiber), 2g pro.

HOW TO MAKE CARAMEL APPLES

Farm-fresh apples are tempting on their own but they're impossible to resist when wrapped in sweet caramel. Follow these steps to make your own batch.

STEP 1
Start by removing the stems and thoroughly washing the apples. Store-bought apples can have a bit of a waxy coating to keep them fresh, so be sure to scrub them until that finish is gone and they look natural and dull. A dishcloth should do the job. Once they're clean, dry the apples and insert a wooden pop stick into the top of each. Line a baking sheet with a piece of greased parchment or waxed paper. (Greasing the paper is an important step, so the caramel won't stick later.) Set the baking sheet on a counter close to the stovetop.

STEP 2
Next, prepare the caramels for all that sticky goodness. Unwrap the candies—this is a great job for the little ones—and heat the caramels in a saucepan with the sweetened condensed milk over medium-low heat, stirring frequently. It should take 3-5 minutes for the mix to become smooth. Once the texture is right, remove from the heat and prepare for dipping. To fully coat the apple, tip the saucepan a bit and rotate the apple until the surface is completely covered.

STEP 3
Allow the excess caramel to drip off before you place the apple upright onto the paper-lined pan. If you find that the caramel runs off the apples, don't worry! It might just be a touch too warm. Wait a minute and give the apple another dip.

STEP 4
Place all the apples on your lined baking sheet. If you're looking to gobble up these sweet treats right away, let the apples stand until the caramel is set, about 10 minutes. Or, you can refrigerate them for a week or so—just be sure to take them out of the fridge 10-15 minutes before eating so the caramel can soften a bit before you take that first bite.

AUTUMN HARVEST PUMPKIN PIE

This is the best pumpkin pie I've ever tasted. Canned
pumpkin speeds things up a bit when you need to save time.

—Stan Strom, Gilbert, AZ

PREP: 30 MIN. + CHILLING • BAKE: 55 MIN. + COOLING • MAKES: 8 SERVINGS

- 2 **cups all-purpose flour**
- 1 **cup cake flour**
- 2 **Tbsp. sugar**
- ½ **tsp. salt**
- ½ **cup cold unsalted
  butter, cubed**
- ½ **cup butter-flavored
  shortening**
- 1 **large egg**
- ⅓ **cup cold water**
- 1 **Tbsp. cider vinegar**

FILLING
- 2½ **cups canned pumpkin
  (about 19 oz.)**
- 1¼ **cups packed light
  brown sugar**
- ¾ **cup half-and-half cream**
- 2 **large eggs**
- ¼ **cup apple butter**
- 2 **Tbsp. orange juice**
- 2 **Tbsp. maple syrup**
- 2 **tsp. ground cinnamon**
- 2 **tsp. pumpkin pie spice**
- ¼ **tsp. salt**

1. In a large bowl, mix first 4 ingredients; cut in the butter and shortening until crumbly. Whisk together egg, water and vinegar; gradually add to flour mixture, tossing with a fork until dough holds together when pressed. Divide the dough in half so that 1 portion is slightly larger than the other; shape each into a disk. Wrap; refrigerate 1 hour or overnight.

2. Preheat oven to 425°. On a lightly floured surface, roll larger portion to a ⅛-in.-thick circle; transfer to a 9-in. deep-dish pie plate. Trim crust to ½ in. beyond edge of pie plate. Refrigerate until ready to fill.

3. Roll smaller portion of dough to ⅛-in. thickness. Cut with a small floured pumpkin-shaped cookie cutter; place some cutouts 1 in. apart on a baking sheet, reserving unbaked cutouts for decorative edge if desired. Bake until golden brown, 8-10 minutes.

4. Meanwhile, beat together filling ingredients until blended; transfer to crust. Flute or decorate edge with unbaked cutouts, brushing off flour before pressing lightly onto edge. Bake on a lower oven rack 10 minutes. Cover edge loosely with foil. Reduce oven setting to 350°. Bake until a knife inserted near the center comes out clean, 45-50 minutes.

5. Cool on a wire rack; serve or refrigerate within 2 hours. Top with baked pumpkin cutouts before serving.

NOTE: This recipe was tested with commercially prepared apple butter.

1 PIECE: 647 cal., 28g fat (12g sat. fat), 112mg chol., 277mg sod., 89g carb. (47g sugars, 4g fiber), 9g pro.

Gather Around the Bonfire

Cheese & Pimiento Spread

Favorite Hot Chocolate

Grandma's Classic
Potato Salad

Watermelon &
Cucumber Salsa

Swiss Cherry Bruschetta

S'mores Cupcakes

Brownie Bourbon Bites

CHEESE & PIMIENTO SPREAD

My mother made delicious pimiento cheese, but this is a spicy, modern version
of her recipe. Serve it stuffed in celery or spread on crackers or a sandwich.

—*Elizabeth Hester, Elizabethtown, NC*

TAKES: 15 MIN. • **MAKES:** 2¾ CUPS

12 oz. sharp white
   cheddar cheese
8 oz. reduced-fat cream
   cheese, softened
2 tsp. Worcestershire
   sauce
2 tsp. white vinegar
¼ tsp. white pepper
¼ tsp. garlic powder
¼ tsp. cayenne pepper
1 jar (4 oz.) diced
   pimientos, undrained
   Assorted crackers and
   vegetables

Shred the cheddar cheese; transfer to a large bowl. Add cream
cheese, Worcestershire sauce, vinegar, pepper, garlic powder
and cayenne; beat on low speed until blended. Drain pimientos,
reserving 2 Tbsp. juice. Stir in pimientos and reserved juice.
Serve with crackers and vegetables.

2 TBSP.: 90 cal., 7g fat (4g sat. fat), 23mg chol., 150mg sod., 1g carb.
(1g sugars, 0 fiber), 5g pro.

KITCHEN TIP: Pimiento cheese is a traditional southern cheese
spread that's served as an appetizer or a condiment. Recipes
vary, but it's always made with a sharp cheddar cheese and diced
pimientos, which are mild Spanish red peppers.

SUMMER NIGHT SNUGGLES

Pack blankets inside a basket to
easily tote to the party. Spread
the blankets on the grass or
beach (keeping a safe distance
from the fire), or snuggle up in
one if the night air gets chilly.

FAVORITE HOT CHOCOLATE

You need just a few basic ingredients to stir up this soul-warming sipper. The comforting beverage is smooth and not too sweet, making it just right for a chilly night.

—*Flo Snodderly, North Vernon, IN*

TAKES: 15 MIN. • MAKES: 8 SERVINGS

1 can (14 oz.) sweetened condensed milk
½ cup baking cocoa
6½ cups water
2 tsp. vanilla extract
Optional: Sweetened whipped cream, marshmallows, chocolate syrup and Pirouette cookies

1. Place milk and baking cocoa in a large saucepan; cook and stir over medium heat until blended. Gradually stir in the water; heat through, stirring occasionally.

2. Remove from heat; stir in the vanilla. Add toppings as desired.

1 CUP: 177 cal., 5g fat (3g sat. fat), 17mg chol., 63mg sod., 30g carb. (27g sugars, 1g fiber), 5g pro.

GRANDMA'S CLASSIC POTATO SALAD

When I asked my grandmother how old this recipe was, she told me that her mom used to make it when she was a little girl. It has definitely stood the test of time.

—*Kimberly Wallace, Dennison, OH*

PREP: 25 MIN. • COOK: 20 MIN. + CHILLING • MAKES: 10 SERVINGS

6 medium potatoes, peeled and cubed
¼ cup all-purpose flour
1 Tbsp. sugar
1½ tsp. salt
1 tsp. ground mustard
1 tsp. pepper
¾ cup water
2 large eggs, beaten
¼ cup white vinegar
4 hard-boiled large eggs, divided use
2 celery ribs, chopped
1 medium onion, chopped
Sliced green onions, optional

1. Place potatoes in a large saucepan and cover with water. Bring to a boil. Reduce the heat; cover and cook until tender, 15-20 minutes. Drain and cool to room temperature.

2. Meanwhile, in a small heavy saucepan, combine flour, sugar, salt, mustard and pepper. Gradually stir in water until mixture is smooth. Cook and stir over medium-high heat until thickened and bubbly. Reduce heat; cook and stir 2 minutes longer.

3. Remove from the heat. Stir a small amount of hot mixture into beaten eggs; return all to the pan, stirring constantly. Bring to a gentle boil; cook and stir 2 minutes longer. Remove from the heat and cool completely. Gently stir in vinegar.

4. Chop and refrigerate 1 hard-boiled egg; chop the remaining 3 hard-boiled eggs. In a large bowl, combine the potatoes, celery, chopped onion and eggs; add dressing and stir until blended. Refrigerate until chilled. Garnish with the reserved chopped egg and, if desired, sliced green onions.

¾ CUP: 144 cal., 3g fat (1g sat. fat), 112mg chol., 402mg sod., 23g carb. (3g sugars, 2g fiber), 6g pro. **DIABETIC EXCHANGES:** 1½ starch, ½ fat.

WATERMELON & CUCUMBER SALSA

The combo of watermelon and cucumber may sound unusual—it tastes
anything but! Eat the salsa with chips, or serve it as a topper with
hot dogs or chicken tacos for a refreshing change of pace.

—Suzanne Curletto, Walnut Creek, CA

TAKES: 15 MIN. • **MAKES:** 3 CUPS

1½ **cups seeded chopped
watermelon**
¾ **cup finely chopped
cucumber**
½ **cup finely chopped
sweet onion**
¼ **cup minced fresh cilantro**
1 **jalapeno pepper,
seeded and minced**
2 **Tbsp. lime juice**
¼ **tsp. salt**

In a small bowl, combine all ingredients; refrigerate until
serving.

NOTE: Wear disposable gloves when cutting hot peppers; the oils
can burn skin. Avoid touching your face.

¼ **CUP:** 10 cal., 0 fat (0 sat. fat), 0 chol., 50mg sod., 3g carb.
(2g sugars, 0 fiber), 0 pro. **DIABETIC EXCHANGES:** Free food.

SWISS CHERRY BRUSCHETTA

This recipe is a spinoff of a cherry chicken main dish my husband adores. The combination of sweet, tart and salty flavors provides a contrast that's hard to resist.

—*Shelly Platten, Amherst, WI*

TAKES: 30 MIN. • MAKES: 16 SERVINGS

2   large onions, chopped
1   garlic clove, minced
4   tsp. olive oil
1   Tbsp. balsamic vinegar
1   tsp. brown sugar
½   tsp. garlic salt
2½ cups pitted dark
    sweet cherries,
    coarsely chopped
16 slices French bread
    (½ in. thick),
    lightly toasted
1½ cups shredded
    Swiss cheese
2   Tbsp. minced
    fresh parsley

1. In a large skillet, saute onions and garlic in oil until tender, about 6 minutes. Add the vinegar, brown sugar and garlic salt; reduce heat. Cook until onions are caramelized, 3-4 minutes. Stir in the cherries; cook until sauce is syrupy, about 5 minutes longer.

2. Place toasted bread on a baking sheet; spoon cherry mixture evenly over toast. Sprinkle with cheese and parsley. Broil 3-4 in. from the heat until cheese is melted, 1-2 minutes.

1 PIECE: 115 cal., 4 g fat (2 g sat. fat), 9 mg chol., 154 mg sod., 15 g carb., 1 g fiber, 4 g pro.

S'MORES CUPCAKES

Marshmallow frosting puts these cupcakes over the top. Chocolate bar pieces and graham cracker crumbs on top make them extra indulgent and even more like the real thing—but better!

—Erin Rachwal, Hartland, WI

PREP: 30 MIN. • **BAKE:** 20 MIN. + COOLING • **MAKES:** 2 DOZEN

¾ cup water
¾ cup buttermilk
2 large eggs, room temperature
3 Tbsp. canola oil
1 tsp. vanilla extract
1½ cups all-purpose flour
1½ cups sugar
¾ cup baking cocoa
1½ tsp. baking soda
¾ tsp. salt
¾ tsp. baking powder

FROSTING
1½ cups butter, softened
2 cups confectioners' sugar
½ tsp. vanilla extract
2 jars (7 oz. each) marshmallow creme
2 Tbsp. graham cracker crumbs
2 milk chocolate candy bars (1.55 oz. each)
Optional: Toasted marshmallows and graham cracker pieces

1. Preheat oven to 350°. In a large bowl, beat water, buttermilk, eggs, oil and vanilla until well blended. Combine the flour, sugar, cocoa, baking soda, salt and baking powder; gradually beat into water mixture until blended.

2. Fill paper-lined muffin cups half full. Bake until a toothpick comes out clean, 16-20 minutes. Cool in pans 10 minutes before removing from pans to wire racks to cool completely.

3. For frosting, in a large bowl, beat the butter until fluffy; beat in the confectioners' sugar and vanilla until smooth. Add the marshmallow creme; beat until light and fluffy. Spread or pipe frosting over cupcakes. Sprinkle with cracker crumbs. Break each candy bar into 12 pieces; garnish cupcakes. If desired, top with toasted marshmallows and graham cracker pieces.

1 CUPCAKE: 330 cal., 15g fat (8g sat. fat), 47mg chol., 298mg sod., 43g carb. (35g sugars, 1g fiber), 3g pro.

TIN CAN LANTERN

Upcycle an empty tin can into a twinkling outdoor lantern. Using a drill or hammer and nails, drill or punch holes into the can. You can create a decorative design if you'd like. Place a votive candle on the inside for a warm glow. Be sure to place the can on a firesafe surface and do not leave a lit votive unattended.

SPARKLER STATION

Use a galvanized metal bucket to house sparklers that guests can grab at their convenience. Then get ready to light up the night!

BROWNIE BOURBON BITES

Chocolate and chopped pecans flavor these simple, spirited treats.
Make a double batch so you can give some away and savor the rest!

—Paula Kirchenbauer, Newton, NJ

PREP: 25 MIN. + CHILLING • **BAKE:** 10 MIN. + COOLING • **MAKES:** ABOUT 2 DOZEN

½ cup butter, softened
½ cup packed brown sugar
¼ cup bourbon
1 cup all-purpose flour
3 Tbsp. baking cocoa
½ cup miniature semisweet
     chocolate chips
1 cup coarsely
     chopped pecans

1. In a small bowl, cream butter and brown sugar until light and fluffy, 5-7 minutes. Beat in the bourbon. Combine the flour and cocoa; gradually add to creamed mixture, beating until smooth. Stir in chocolate chips. Cover and refrigerate for 1-2 hours.

2. Shape into 1-in. balls; roll in pecans. Place 2 in. apart on ungreased baking sheets. Bake at 350° until the cookies are set, 8-10 minutes. Cool for 5 minutes before carefully removing from the pans to wire racks to cool completely. Store in an airtight container.

1 COOKIE: 110 cal., 7g fat (3g sat. fat), 9mg chol., 35mg sod., 10g carb. (6g sugars, 1g fiber), 1g pro.

Halloween in the Country

Pumpkin Herb Rolls

Mummy-Wrapped Brie

Roasted Pumpkin Nachos

Pumpkin Spice Sangria

Crescent Roll Witch Hats

Halloween Party
Cutout Cookies

Jack-o'-Lantern Cake

PUMPKIN HERB ROLLS

These cute pumpkin rolls are worth the effort. They're a festive fall favorite in my household. If you don't have pumpkin on hand, try using sweet potato.

—*Veronica Fay, Knoxville, TN*

PREP: 1 HOUR + RISING • **BAKE:** 15 MIN. + COOLING • **MAKES:** 1 DOZEN

1 Tbsp. active dry yeast
¾ cup warm water (110° to 115°)
¾ cup canned pumpkin
2 tsp. garlic powder
2 tsp. onion powder
2 Tbsp. dried minced onion
1½ tsp. each minced fresh oregano, sage, rosemary and thyme
1 tsp. salt
¼ tsp. cayenne pepper
2¾ to 3¼ cups bread flour
2 cups shredded sharp cheddar cheese
¼ cup butter, melted, optional
6 honey wheat braided pretzel twists, halved

1. In a small bowl, dissolve yeast in warm water. In a large bowl, combine pumpkin, garlic powder, onion powder, dried onion, fresh herbs, salt, cayenne, yeast mixture and 1½ cups flour; beat on medium speed until smooth. Stir in enough remaining flour to form a soft dough (dough will be sticky). Stir in cheese.

2. Turn dough onto a floured surface; knead until smooth and elastic, 6-8 minutes. Place in a greased bowl, turning once to grease the top. Cover and let rise in a warm place until doubled, about 1½ hours.

3. Punch down the dough; turn onto a lightly floured surface. Divide and shape into 12 balls; flatten slightly. Wrap each ball in 4 pieces of kitchen string, creating indentions to resemble a pumpkin. Place 2 in. apart on greased baking sheets. Cover with kitchen towels; let rise in a warm place until almost doubled, about 45 minutes.

4. Preheat oven to 375°. Bake until golden brown, 15-20 minutes. If desired, brush with melted butter. Remove from pans to wire racks to cool. Cut and discard string. Before serving, insert pretzel halves in top of each roll.

1 ROLL: 211 cal., 7g fat (4g sat. fat), 19mg chol., 348mg sod., 28g carb. (1g sugars, 2g fiber), 9g pro.

MUMMY-WRAPPED BRIE

You can assemble our baked Brie appetizer in advance and bake it right before the party.

—Taste of Home *Test Kitchen*

TAKES: 30 MIN. • **MAKES:** 10 SERVINGS

1 pkg. (17.3 oz.) frozen
   puff pastry, thawed
¼ cup apricot jam
1 round (16 oz.) Brie cheese
1 large egg
1 Tbsp. water
   Apple slices
2 dried cranberries
   or raisins

1. Preheat oven to 400°. Unfold 1 sheet of puff pastry. On a lightly floured surface, roll pastry into a 14-in. square. Cut off corners to make a circle. Spread jam into a 4½-in. circle in center of pastry. Place Brie on top; fold pastry over cheese, trimming as necessary, and pinch edges to seal. Beat egg and water; brush over pastry.

2. Place on an ungreased baking sheet, seam side down. Roll remaining pastry into a 14-in. square. Cut four 1-in. strips; cut strips in half crosswise. Wrap strips around Brie, trimming as necessary. Discard scraps. Bake 10 minutes; brush again with egg wash. Bake until golden brown, 10-15 minutes more. For eyes, cut 2 circles from apple slices; place on top of Brie. Top each circle with a dried cranberry. Serve warm, with apple slices.

1 SERVING: 372 cal., 24g fat (10g sat. fat), 64mg chol., 426mg sod., 28g carb. (4g sugars, 3g fiber), 13g pro.

KITCHEN TIP: Use any jam or preserves in place of apricot. We like this with jalapeno or smoky bacon jam.

ROASTED PUMPKIN NACHOS

Previously, I had made this dish with black beans and corn off the cob in the summer. Wanting to try it with fresh fall ingredients, I replaced the corn with roasted pumpkin—yum! It's also good with butternut squash.

—Lesle Harwood, Douglassville, PA

PREP: 40 MIN. • **BAKE:** 10 MIN. • **MAKES:** 12 SERVINGS

4 cups cubed fresh pumpkin or butternut squash (about 1 lb.)
2 Tbsp. olive oil
¼ tsp. salt
⅛ tsp. pepper
1 pkg. (13 oz.) tortilla chips
1 can (15 oz.) black beans, rinsed and drained
1 jar (16 oz.) salsa
3 cups shredded Mexican cheese blend
   Optional toppings: Minced fresh cilantro, sliced green onions and hot pepper sauce

1. Preheat oven to 400°. Place pumpkin in a greased 15x10x1-in. baking pan. Drizzle with oil; sprinkle with salt and pepper. Toss to coat. Roast until tender, 25-30 minutes, stirring occasionally.

2. Reduce oven setting to 350°. On a greased 15x10x1-in. baking pan, layer half each of the chips, beans, pumpkin, salsa and cheese. Repeat layers. Bake 8-10 minutes or until cheese is melted. Add toppings of your choice; serve immediately.

1 SERVING: 347 cal., 18g fat (6g sat. fat), 25mg chol., 559mg sod., 36g carb. (3g sugars, 4g fiber), 10g pro.

UTENSIL PACKETS

Using disposable utensils makes cleanup quick and easy. Fold a napkin in half. Insert napkin and utensils into a waxed paper bag. Fold over the edge of the bag and tie a knot or bow with ribbon around the packet.

PUMPKIN SPICE SANGRIA

This pumpkin sangria is made of sweet white wine, spices, and fresh pears and apples. Using canned pumpkin makes it easy.

—*James Schend, Pleasant Prairie, WI*

PREP: 25 MIN. + CHILLING • **MAKES:** 12 SERVINGS (2¼ QT.)

3 cinnamon sticks (3 in.)
10 whole allspice
10 whole cloves
3 cups water
1 can (15 oz.) canned pumpkin
¼ cup lemon juice
1 bottle (750 ml) sweet white wine
1 cup apple brandy or plain brandy
1 large apple, thinly sliced
1 large pear, thinly sliced

1. Place cinnamon, allspice and cloves on a double thickness of cheesecloth; bring up corners of cloth and tie with string to form a bag.

2. Place water, pumpkin, lemon juice and spice bag in a large saucepan. Bring to a boil. Remove from heat; cover and steep for 5 minutes. Transfer to a pitcher; stir in wine, brandy and fruit. Cover and refrigerate at least 3 hours. Discard spice bag. Stir just before serving.

¾ CUP: 126 cal., 0 fat (0 sat. fat), 0 chol., 5mg sod., 10g carb. (5g sugars, 2g fiber), 1g pro.

RECYCLED SOUP-CAN VASES

Spray-paint clean soup cans
in a ventilated area. Apply 2-3 coats,
allowing about 1 minute between coats.
When completely dry, decorate with ribbon.
Secure ribbon with hot glue.

CRESCENT ROLL WITCH HATS

It doesn't take magic to transform these crescent rolls into charming witch hats—just a few minutes and a couple of ingredients. They're so good, you'll want to make a double batch.

—*Mara Fletcher, Batesville, IN*

TAKES: 25 MIN. • MAKES: 16 ROLLS

2   tubes (8 oz. each) refrigerated crescent rolls
¼   cup butter, softened
¼   cup minced fresh basil
2   Tbsp. oil-packed sun-dried tomatoes, patted dry and finely chopped
½   tsp. garlic powder

1. Preheat oven to 375°. Unroll each tube of crescent dough; separate each dough into 8 triangles. In a small bowl, mix the remaining ingredients. Spread 1 tsp. filling along the wide end of each triangle; carefully roll up once to form brim of hat.

2. Place 2 in. apart on ungreased baking sheets. Bake until golden brown, 10-12 minutes. Rotate halfway through baking to ensure even browning.

1 ROLL: 129 cal., 8g fat (2g sat. fat), 8mg chol., 238mg sod., 12g carb. (3g sugars, 0 fiber), 2g pro.

HALLOWEEN PARTY CUTOUT COOKIES

I've been making these Halloween cookies for about 40 years—first for my children and now my grandchildren and all their friends, too. I make about 20 trays a year to give away to trick-or-treaters.
—*Pamela Shank, Parkersburg, WV*

PREP: 1 HOUR + CHILLING • **BAKE:** 10 MIN./BATCH + COOLING • **MAKES:** 2 DOZEN

½ cup butter, softened
¾ cup sugar
1 large egg, room temperature
1 tsp. vanilla extract
1½ cups all-purpose flour
1 tsp. baking powder
½ tsp. salt

FROSTING
3¾ cups confectioners' sugar
¼ cup shortening
4 to 6 Tbsp. water
Optional: Yellow, orange, green and black paste food coloring

1. In a large bowl, beat butter and sugar until light and blended. Beat in egg and vanilla. In another bowl, whisk flour, baking powder and salt; gradually beat into creamed mixture. Shape the dough into 2 portions. Shape each into a disk; wrap and refrigerate 1 hour or until firm enough to roll.

2. Preheat oven to 350°. On a lightly floured surface, roll each portion of dough to ¼-in. thickness. Cut with floured 2½-in. Halloween-shaped cookie cutters. Place 2 in. apart on ungreased baking sheets. Bake 8-10 minutes or until the edges are light brown. Remove from pans to wire racks to cool completely.

3. In a large bowl, beat confectioners' sugar, shortening and enough water to reach spreading consistency. Tint frosting and decorate as desired. Let stand until set.

1 COOKIE: 182 cal., 6g fat (3g sat. fat), 18mg chol., 103mg sod., 31g carb. (25g sugars, 0 fiber), 1g pro.

JACK-O'-LANTERN CAKE

I pieced two fluted tube pan cakes together to make this gap-toothed grinner.
It'll make the best-ever centerpiece at your Halloween party.
—*Julianne Johnson, Grove City, MN*

PREP: 35 MIN. • BAKE: 30 MIN. + COOLING • MAKES: 16 SERVINGS

2 **pkg. spice cake mix
   (regular size)**
4 **cans (16 oz. each)
   vanilla frosting
   Red and yellow food
   coloring**
1 **ice cream cake cone
   (about 3 in. tall)**
2 **Oreo cookies**
1 **pkg. (24 oz.) ready-to-use
   rolled black fondant**

1. Prepare and bake cakes according to package directions using two 10-in. fluted tube pans. Invert cakes onto wire racks; cool completely. Meanwhile, tint frosting orange using red and yellow food coloring.

2. Cut a thin slice off bottom of each cake. Spread 1 cake bottom with frosting; press the flat sides together to make a pumpkin shape. Place a foil ball in the center to support the stem; top with an ice cream cake cone. Frost cake with the remaining frosting.

3. To decorate face, roll out fondant to ⅛-in. thickness; cut into desired shapes for mouth and nose. Remove tops from 2 Oreo cookies; cut half-circles in filling for eyes. Press cookies and fondant into frosting to make the face.

1 PIECE: 985 cal., 33g fat (12g sat. fat), 70mg chol., 709mg sod., 166g carb. (128g sugars, 0 fiber), 5g pro.

Down-Home Thanksgiving

Brined Grilled Turkey Breast

Cider Baked Squash

Triple-Cheese Broccoli Puff

Duo Tater Bake

Maple-Gingerroot Vegetables

Buttermilk Biscuits

Hot Cider

Bourbon Brioche Bread Pudding

BRINED GRILLED TURKEY BREAST

You'll want to give thanks for this mouthwatering turkey! Moist and slightly sweet, with just a hint of spice, it's one of our best turkey recipes ever.
—*Tina Mirilovich, Johnstown, PA*

PREP: 20 MIN. + MARINATING • GRILL: 1¼ HOURS + STANDING • **MAKES:** 6 SERVINGS

2 qt. cold water, divided
½ cup kosher salt
½ cup packed brown sugar
1 Tbsp. whole peppercorns
1 boneless skinless turkey breast half (2 to 3 lbs.)

BASTING SAUCE
¼ cup canola oil
¼ cup sesame oil
¼ cup reduced-sodium soy sauce
3 Tbsp. lemon juice
2 Tbsp. honey
3 garlic cloves, minced
¼ tsp. dried thyme
¼ tsp. crushed red pepper flakes

1. In a large saucepan, combine 1 qt. water, salt, brown sugar and peppercorns. Bring to a boil. Cook and stir until salt and sugar are dissolved. Pour into a large bowl. Add remaining 1 qt. cold water to cool the brine to room temperature. Add turkey breast; turn to coat. Cover and refrigerate 4-6 hours, turning occasionally.

2. Prepare grill for indirect medium heat, using a drip pan. Meanwhile, combine basting sauce ingredients. Grill turkey, covered, until a thermometer reads 170°, 1¼-1½ hours, basting occasionally with sauce. Remove to a cutting board. Cover and let stand 10 minutes before slicing.

NOTE: This recipe was tested with Morton brand kosher salt. It is best not to use a prebasted turkey breast for this recipe.

5 OZ. COOKED TURKEY: 364 cal., 19g fat (2g sat. fat), 94mg chol., 553mg sod., 8g carb. (6g sugars, 0 fiber), 38g pro.

CIDER BAKED SQUASH

I'm a freelance writer who sometimes needs a break from a long session of working on a story. That's when I escape to the kitchen to whip up something that's good to eat, yet easy to prepare. This is one of my favorites!

—Christine Gibson, Fontana, WI

PREP: 15 MIN. • **BAKE:** 40 MIN. • **MAKES:** 6 SERVINGS

2 medium acorn squash, cut into 1-in. slices, seeds removed
½ cup apple cider or juice
¼ cup packed brown sugar
½ tsp. salt
⅛ tsp. ground cinnamon
⅛ tsp. ground mace

Preheat oven to 325° Arrange squash in a 15x10x1-in. baking pan. Pour cider over squash. Combine the brown sugar, salt, cinnamon and mace; sprinkle over squash. Cover with foil. Bake until squash is tender, 40-45 minutes.

2 PIECES: 137 cal., 0 fat (0 sat. fat), 0 chol., 208mg sod., 35g carb. (16g sugars, 3g fiber), 2g pro. **DIABETIC EXCHANGES:** 2 starch.

PLACE OF GRACE UTENSIL HOLDERS

Set out these simple paper utensil holders with a pencil or pen at each place setting so your guests can reflect on the year's blessings.

STEP 1
Fold up one end of the paper about 5 in. so the short end of the fold is on top.

STEP 2
Measure 2¼ in. in from each side; mark lightly with pencil. Fold flaps back at measured marks, making a 4-in.-wide front pocket. Overlap the flaps at back and secure with tape or a sticker.

STEP 3
Use letter stamps—or your best penmanship—to write "Count Your Blessings" near the top edge of the pocket. Add numerals to form a list.

STEP 4
Using a ruler as guide, make dotted lines next to each numeral with a fine-tip marker. Stamp a decoration near the bottom of the pocket if desired.

STEP 5
Insert silverware into pocket. Set utensil holder near place setting along with a pencil or pen.

☐ 8½x11-in. writing or decorative paper

☐ Stamps (letter, numeral and optional decorative) and stamp pad

TRIPLE-CHEESE BROCCOLI PUFF

This rich-tasting side dish is a must for our special menus. Like any puffy souffle,
it will settle a bit after you remove it from the oven, but the pretty golden top is very attractive.
—*Maryellen Hays, Wolcottville, IN*

PREP: 15 MIN. • **BAKE:** 50 MIN. + STANDING • **MAKES:** 8 SERVINGS

1 cup sliced fresh
  mushrooms
1 Tbsp. butter
3 oz. cream cheese,
  softened
6 large eggs, room
  temperature
1 cup 2% milk
¾ cup biscuit/baking mix
3 cups frozen chopped
  broccoli, thawed
2 cups shredded
  Monterey Jack cheese
1 cup 4% cottage cheese
¼ tsp. salt

SERVE IT WITH:
Mustard Cranberry
Glazed Ham, Page 55

1. In a small skillet, saute mushrooms in butter until tender. In a large bowl, beat the cream cheese, eggs, milk and biscuit mix just until combined. Stir in the broccoli, cheeses, salt and mushrooms.

2. Pour into a greased 2½-qt. baking dish. Bake, uncovered, at 350° until a thermometer reads 160°, 50-60 minutes. Let stand for 10 minutes before serving.

1 SERVING: 315 cal., 21g fat (12g sat. fat), 210mg chol., 578mg sod., 13g carb. (4g sugars, 1g fiber), 19g pro.

KITCHEN TIP: It's easy to turn this cheesy side dish into an entree. Simply stir in cooked ham or chicken when adding the broccoli to the egg mixture.

DUO TATER BAKE

Cut down on holiday prep time with this creamy potato dish that combines sweet potatoes with regular spuds. I served this for Thanksgiving, and it was a winner with my family.

—Joan McCulloch, Abbotsford, BC

PREP: 40 MIN. • BAKE: 20 MIN. • MAKES: 2 CASSEROLES (10 SERVINGS EACH)

4 lbs. russet or Yukon
    Gold potatoes,
    peeled and cubed
3 lbs. sweet potatoes,
    peeled and cubed
2 cartons (8 oz. each)
    spreadable chive
    and onion cream
    cheese, divided
1 cup sour cream, divided
¼ cup shredded Colby-
    Monterey Jack cheese
⅓ cup 2% milk
¼ cup shredded
    Parmesan cheese
½ tsp. salt
½ tsp. pepper

TOPPING
1 cup shredded Colby-
    Monterey Jack cheese
½ cup chopped
    green onions
¼ cup shredded
    Parmesan cheese

1. Place russet potatoes in a Dutch oven and cover with water. Bring to a boil. Reduce heat; cover and cook for 10-15 minutes or until tender.

2. Meanwhile, place sweet potatoes in a large saucepan; cover with water. Bring to a boil. Reduce heat; cover and cook until tender, 10-15 minutes. Drain; mash with half of the cream cheese and sour cream, and the Colby-Monterey Jack cheese.

3. Drain russet potatoes; mash with the remaining cream cheese and sour cream. Stir in the milk, Parmesan cheese, salt and pepper.

4. Spread 1⅓ cups russet potato mixture into each of 2 greased 11x7-in. baking dishes. Layer each with 2 cups sweet potato mixture. Repeat layers. Spread with the remaining russet potato mixture.

5. Bake, uncovered, at 350° until heated through, about 15 minutes. Combine topping ingredients; sprinkle over casseroles. Bake until cheese is melted, 2-3 minutes longer.

¾ CUP: 236 cal., 12g fat (8g sat. fat), 38mg chol., 246mg sod., 25g carb. (7g sugars, 2g fiber), 5g pro.

MAPLE-GINGERROOT VEGETABLES

My family loves the drizzling of golden maple syrup on these roasted vegetables. I prefer to use dark maple syrup. Either way, it's an easy way to get kids (and adults) to eat their veggies.

—*Kelli Ritz, Innisfail, AB*

PREP: 35 MIN. • BAKE: 45 MIN. • MAKES: 24 SERVINGS

5   medium parsnips, peeled and sliced
5   small carrots, sliced
3   medium turnips, peeled and cubed
1   large sweet potato, peeled and cubed
1   small rutabaga, peeled and cubed
1   large sweet onion, cut into wedges
1   small red onion, cut into wedges
2   Tbsp. olive oil
1   Tbsp. minced fresh gingerroot
1   tsp. salt
½   tsp. pepper
1   cup maple syrup

1. Place the first 7 ingredients in a large bowl; add the oil, ginger, salt and pepper. Toss to coat. Arrange vegetables in a single layer in two 15x10x1-in. baking pans coated with cooking spray.

2. Bake, uncovered, at 425° for 25 minutes, stirring once. Drizzle with syrup. Bake until vegetables are tender, 20-25 minutes longer, stirring once more.

¾ CUP: 92 cal., 1g fat (0 sat. fat), 0 chol., 119mg sod., 20g carb. (13g sugars, 2g fiber), 1g pro. **DIABETIC EXCHANGES:** 1 starch.

KITCHEN TIP: Sweeten the deal by adding a small chopped apple to the veggie mixture.

BUTTERMILK BISCUITS

These biscuits are made from a recipe that's been in our family for years. They're simple to make and smell so good when baking! The wonderful aroma takes me back to those days when Mom made these—it's like I'm there in our family's kitchen again, with her busy at the stove.

—Jean Parsons, Sarver, PA

PREP: 25 MIN. • BAKE: 15 MIN. • MAKES: 1½ DOZEN

2 cups all-purpose flour
1 Tbsp. sugar
1 tsp. baking powder
½ tsp. salt
½ tsp. baking soda
¼ cup cold shortening
¾ cup buttermilk

1. Preheat oven to 450°. In a large bowl, combine the flour, sugar, baking powder, salt and baking soda. Cut in shortening until mixture resembles coarse crumbs. Add buttermilk; stir just until the dough clings together.

2. Turn onto a lightly floured surface; knead gently, 10-12 times. Roll to ½-in. thickness; cut with a floured 2-in. round biscuit cutter. Place 1 in. apart on a greased baking sheet. Bake until lightly browned, 11-12 minutes. Serve warm.

1 BISCUIT: 82 cal., 3g fat (1g sat. fat), 0 chol., 147mg sod., 12g carb. (1g sugars, 0 fiber), 2g pro.

BOURBON BRIOCHE BREAD PUDDING

My husband wasn't a fan of bread pudding until I had him try a bite of mine from a local restaurant. I replicated it with some added bourbon, walnuts and a different type of bread. It's a keeper!

—Cindy Worth, Lapwai, ID

PREP: 25 MIN. + STANDING • **BAKE:** 35 MIN. • **MAKES:** 6 SERVINGS

½ cup bourbon, divided
½ cup raisins
2½ cups brioche
   bread, toasted
⅓ cup finely chopped
   walnuts
4 large eggs
1¾ cups heavy
   whipping cream
⅓ cup sugar
1 tsp. ground cinnamon
1 tsp. vanilla extract
½ tsp. ground nutmeg
¼ tsp. salt
   Optional: Confectioners'
   sugar and whipped
   cream

1. Preheat oven to 375°. Pour ¼ cup bourbon over raisins in a small bowl; let stand 5 minutes. Place bread in a greased 8-in. square baking dish. Top with walnuts, raisins and soaking liquid.

2. In a large bowl, whisk eggs, cream, sugar, cinnamon, vanilla, nutmeg, salt and remaining bourbon until blended. Pour over bread; let stand until bread is softened, about 15 minutes.

3. Bake, uncovered, until puffed, golden and a knife inserted in the center comes out clean, 35-40 minutes. Serve warm. If desired, serve with confectioners' sugar and whipped cream.

1 SERVING: 469 cal., 34g fat (19g sat. fat), 213mg chol., 218mg sod., 30g carb. (22g sugars, 1g fiber), 9g pro.

HOT CIDER

I dress up traditional apple cider using lemonade, orange juice, honey and spices. It's a new version of a classic fall beverage.

—*Glenna Tooman, Boise, ID*

PREP: 5 MIN. • **COOK:** 45 MIN. • **MAKES:** 18 SERVINGS (4½ QT.)

4 cups water
2 tsp. ground allspice
1 cinnamon stick (3 in.)
  Dash ground cloves
1 gallon apple cider or unsweetened apple juice
1 can (12 oz.) frozen lemonade concentrate, thawed
¾ cup orange juice
⅓ cup honey
1 tea bag
  Apple slices, optional

1. In a stockpot, combine the water, allspice, cinnamon stick and cloves. Bring to a boil. Reduce heat; simmer, uncovered, for 30 minutes.

2. Add the next 5 ingredients. Return just to a boil. Discard cinnamon stick and tea bag. Stir and serve warm. If desired, garnish with apple slices.

1 CUP: 168 cal., 0 fat (0 sat. fat), 0 chol., 24mg sod., 42g carb. (38g sugars, 0 fiber), 0 pro.

Kids' Thanksgiving Table

Gobbler Goodies
•••
Oven Chicken Fingers
•••
Baked Corn Pudding
•••
Fluffy Caramel Apple Dip
•••
Bacon Cheeseburger Buns
•••
Cheddar Buttermilk Biscuits
•••
Turkey Macaroni Bake
•••
Maple Tree Cake

GOBBLER GOODIES

The kids and I had a ball making these tasty "turkeys" for Thanksgiving one year. The treats would make fun favors at each place setting—if your family doesn't gobble them up first!
—*Sue Gronholz, Beaver Dam, WI*

PREP: 30 MIN. • **COOK:** 5 MIN. + COOLING • **MAKES:** 28 SERVINGS

¼ cup butter, cubed
4 cups miniature
    marshmallows
6 cups crisp rice cereal
28 chocolate sandwich
    cookies
1½ cups chocolate frosting
1 pkg. (11 oz.) candy corn
28 malted milk balls
    White candy coating,
    optional

1. In a large saucepan, melt butter. Add marshmallows; stir over low heat until melted. Stir in cereal. Cool for 10 minutes. With buttered hands, form cereal mixture into 1½-in. balls. Twist apart sandwich cookies. If desired, remove filling and save for another use. Spread frosting over each cookie half.

2. Place 28 cookie halves under cereal balls to form the base for each turkey. Place 5 pieces of candy corn in a fan pattern on remaining cookie halves; press each half onto a cereal ball to form the tail. Attach remaining candy corn with frosting to form turkey wings. For head, attach a malted milk ball with frosting; cut the white tip off additional candy and attach to head with frosting to form beak. If desired, place melted white candy coating in a piping bag fitted with a #1 round tip; pipe onto head to form eyes. Allow to stand until frosting has set. Store, tightly covered, at room temperature.

1 PIECE: 222 cal., 6g fat (2g sat. fat), 0 chol., 125mg sod., 43g carb. (31g sugars, 1g fiber), 1g pro.

OVEN CHICKEN FINGERS

Youngsters go crazy for chicken fingers, and they're sure to love these
tender, golden strips with two tempting sauces for dipping.

—*Mary Peterson, Charlestown, RI*

PREP: 15 MIN. • BAKE: 20 MIN. • MAKES: 6 SERVINGS

1 cup Italian bread crumbs
2 Tbsp. grated
  Parmesan cheese
1 garlic clove, minced
¼ cup vegetable oil
6 boneless skinless
  chicken breast
  halves (5 oz. each)

CRANBERRY ORANGE SAUCE
¼ cup sugar
2 tsp. cornstarch
½ cup fresh or frozen
  cranberries
½ cup orange juice
¼ cup water

HONEY MUSTARD SAUCE
2 Tbsp. cornstarch
1 cup water, divided
½ cup honey
¼ cup prepared mustard

1. Preheat oven to 375°. In a shallow dish, combine bread
crumbs and Parmesan cheese; set aside. In a small bowl,
combine garlic and oil. Flatten chicken to ½-in. thickness; cut
into 1-in.-wide strips. Dip strips in oil; coat with crumb mixture.
Place on a greased baking sheet. Bake until golden brown,
20-25 minutes.

2. Meanwhile, for cranberry sauce, combine the sugar and
cornstarch in a saucepan. Add cranberries, orange juice and
water; bring to a boil over medium heat, stirring constantly.
Cook and stir 2-3 minutes more, crushing berries while stirring.

3. For honey mustard sauce, dissolve cornstarch in 1 Tbsp.
water in a saucepan. Add honey, mustard and remaining water;
bring to a boil over medium heat. Boil for 1 minute, stirring
constantly. Serve with chicken for dipping.

1 SERVING: 458 cal., 14g fat (2g sat. fat), 80mg chol., 490mg sod.,
52g carb. (35g sugars, 1g fiber), 32g pro.

MAYFLOWER MIX
A chocolate-dipped waffle cone
filled with trail mix gives little
turkeys a fun snack to munch on
before the big feast begins.

BAKED CORN PUDDING

Here's a comforting side dish the little ones will eat by the spoonful. A holiday favorite with our entire family, it tastes as sweet and creamy as custard. Our guests love it just as much as we do.
—*Peggy West, Georgetown, DE*

PREP: 10 MIN. • **BAKE:** 45 MIN. • **MAKES:** 10 SERVINGS

½ cup sugar
3 Tbsp. all-purpose flour
3 large eggs
1 cup whole milk
¼ cup butter, melted
½ tsp. salt
½ tsp. pepper
1 can (15¼ oz.) whole kernel corn, drained
1 can (14¾ oz.) cream-style corn

1. In a large bowl, combine sugar and flour. Whisk in the eggs, milk, butter, salt and pepper. Stir in the corn and cream-style corn.

2. Pour into a greased 1½-qt. baking dish. Bake, uncovered, at 350° for 45-50 minutes or until a knife inserted in the center comes out clean.

½ CUP: 186 cal., 7g fat (4g sat. fat), 79mg chol., 432mg sod., 26g carb. (14g sugars, 1g fiber), 4g pro.

FLUFFY CARAMEL APPLE DIP

This sweet, smooth and fluffy dip is really a crowd-pleaser.
Be careful—it's so good that you won't want to stop eating it!
—Taste of Home *Test Kitchen*

TAKES: 30 MIN. • **MAKES:** 2 CUPS

1 pkg. (8 oz.) cream cheese, softened
½ cup packed brown sugar
¼ cup caramel ice cream topping
1 tsp. vanilla extract
1 cup marshmallow creme
Apple slices

In a small bowl, beat cream cheese, brown sugar, caramel topping and vanilla until smooth; fold in marshmallow creme. Serve with apple slices.

2 TBSP.: 110 cal., 5g fat (3g sat. fat), 14mg chol., 69mg sod., 15g carb. (14g sugars, 0 fiber), 1g pro.

BACON CHEESEBURGER BUNS

Here's a fun way to serve bacon cheeseburgers to a group without all the fuss of assembling sandwiches. Serve ketchup or barbecue sauce on the side for dipping.

—*Marjorie Miller, Haven, KS*

PREP: 1 HOUR + RISING • **BAKE:** 10 MIN. • **MAKES:** 2 DOZEN

2 pkg. (¼ oz. each) active dry yeast

⅔ cup warm water (110° to 115°)

⅔ cup warm 2% milk (110° to 115°)

¼ cup sugar

¼ cup shortening

2 large eggs, room temperature

2 tsp. salt

4½ to 5 cups all-purpose flour

FILLING

1 lb. sliced bacon, diced

2 lbs. ground beef

1 small onion, chopped

1½ tsp. salt

½ tsp. pepper

1 lb. Velveeta, cubed

3 to 4 Tbsp. butter, melted
Optional: Sesame seeds and ketchup or barbecue sauce

1. In a large bowl, dissolve yeast in warm water. Add milk, sugar, shortening, eggs, salt and 3½ cups flour; beat until smooth. Stir in enough remaining flour to form a soft dough.

2. Turn onto a floured surface; knead until smooth and elastic, 6-8 minutes. Place in a greased bowl, turning once to grease top. Cover and let rise in a warm place until doubled, about 1 hour.

3. Meanwhile, in a large skillet, cook bacon over medium heat until crisp. Using a slotted spoon, remove to paper towels. In a Dutch oven, cook the beef, onion, salt and pepper over medium heat until meat is no longer pink; drain. Add bacon and cheese; cook and stir until cheese is melted. Remove from the heat.

4. Preheat oven to 400°. Punch dough down. Turn onto a lightly floured surface; divide into fourths. Roll each portion into an 12x8-in. rectangle; cut each into 6 squares. Place ¼ cup meat mixture in the center of each square. Bring corners together in the center and pinch to seal.

5. Place 2 in. apart on greased baking sheets. Bake until lightly browned, 9-11 minutes. Brush with butter. If desired, sprinkle with sesame seeds and serve with ketchup.

1 BUN: 310 cal., 17g fat (7g sat. fat), 68mg chol., 720mg sod., 22g carb. (4g sugars, 1g fiber), 16g pro.

CHEDDAR BUTTERMILK BISCUITS

Every bite of these flaky biscuits gets a little kick from cayenne pepper and sharp cheddar cheese. They're a nice accompaniment to a holiday meal.

—*Kimberly Nuttall, San Marcos, CA*

PREP: 20 MIN. • BAKE: 15 MIN. • MAKES: 7 BISCUITS

2 cups all-purpose flour
2 Tbsp. sugar
4 tsp. baking powder
½ tsp. salt
¼ to ½ tsp. cayenne pepper
½ cup cold butter, cubed
½ cup shredded sharp cheddar cheese
¾ cup buttermilk

1. In a large bowl, combine the flour, sugar, baking powder, salt and cayenne. Cut in butter until the mixture resembles coarse crumbs. Add the cheese and toss. Stir in buttermilk just until moistened.

2. Turn dough onto a lightly floured surface; knead 8-10 times. Pat or roll to 1 in. thickness; cut with a floured 2½-in. biscuit cutter. Place biscuits 1 in. apart in a large ungreased cast-iron or other ovenproof skillet. Bake at 425° until golden brown, 15-18 minutes. Serve warm.

1 BISCUIT: 304 cal., 16g fat (10g sat. fat), 44mg chol., 651mg sod., 32g carb. (5g sugars, 1g fiber), 7g pro.

MATERIALS

☐ Multicolored construction paper
☐ Black marker
☐ Kid-safe scissors
☐ Pairs of googly eyes
☐ Liquid glue
☐ Pine cones

PINE CONE TURKEYS

Encourage an atmosphere of gratitude this Thanksgiving with a fun and easy craft that will keep little hands busy.

STEP 1
Have the kids trace their hands onto multicolored construction paper.

STEP 2
Cut out the hand shapes, leaves and a small orange triangle for the turkey beak.

STEP 3
Ask each child to write something they are thankful for onto leaf and hand cutouts.

STEP 4
Use liquid glue to attach 2 googly eyes and a beak to each of the pine cones.

STEP 5
Use additional glue to attach the leaves or hand shape to the back of each pine cone for feathers.

NOTE
Assist the children, especially younger ones, as needed.

TURKEY MACARONI BAKE

A co-worker gave me this recipe when we were discussing quick and easy ways to use leftover turkey. The mild, cheesy casserole is a hit with my family. And it doesn't get much easier than this—you don't even have to cook the macaroni first!

—Cherry Williams, St. Albert, AB

PREP: 15 MIN. • **BAKE:** 65 MIN. • **MAKES:** 6 SERVINGS

2 cups cubed cooked turkey
1½ cups uncooked elbow macaroni
2 cups shredded cheddar cheese, divided
1 can (10¾ oz.) condensed cream of chicken soup, undiluted
1 cup 2% milk
1 can (8 oz.) mushroom stems and pieces, drained
¼ tsp. pepper

1. Preheat oven to 350°. In a large bowl, combine turkey, macaroni, 1½ cups cheese, soup, milk, mushrooms and pepper. Pour into a greased 2-qt. baking dish.

2. Cover and bake 60-65 minutes or until the macaroni is tender. Uncover; sprinkle with the remaining ½ cup cheese. Bake until cheese is melted, 5-10 minutes longer.

1¼ CUPS: 359 cal., 18g fat (11g sat. fat), 85mg chol., 804mg sod., 21g carb. (3g sugars, 2g fiber), 28g pro.

THE GRATEFUL PUMPKIN

A plain white pumpkin makes the perfect canvas for thankful thoughts from all your guests. It's a happy display of the good things in life that lasts until the leftovers head home.

MAPLE TREE CAKE

The kids—and grown-ups, too!—will go crazy for this cute-as-can-be cake.
A chocolate-peanut butter tree with pretty colorful leaves tops off the maple-flavored cake.
—*Lorraine Tishmack, Casselton, ND*

PREP: 25 MIN. • BAKE: 30 MIN. + COOLING • MAKES: 16 SERVINGS

4 large eggs, room
temperature
2 cups sugar
2 cups sour cream
2 tsp. maple flavoring
2½ cups all-purpose flour
2 tsp. baking soda
Dash salt
½ cup chopped pecans

FROSTING
6 Tbsp. butter, softened
4½ cups confectioners' sugar
¾ cup plus 2 Tbsp.
maple syrup
¼ cup semisweet
chocolate chips
¼ cup peanut butter chips
½ tsp. red paste
food coloring
¼ tsp. yellow paste
food coloring

1. Preheat oven to 350°. In a large bowl, beat eggs and sugar. Add sour cream and maple flavoring. Combine flour, baking soda and salt; add to sour cream mixture and mix well. Fold in pecans.

2. Pour into 2 greased and floured 9-in. round baking pans. Bake until a toothpick inserted in the center comes out clean, about 30 minutes. Cool 10 minutes before removing from pans to wire racks to cool completely.

3. For frosting, in a bowl, cream butter and confectioners' sugar. Add syrup; mix well. Set aside ⅔ cup frosting for decoration. Spread remaining frosting between layers and over top and sides of cake.

4. In a microwave-safe bowl, melt chocolate and peanut butter chips; stir until smooth. Transfer to a pastry bag or heavy-duty resealable plastic bag; cut a small hole in the corner of the bag. Pipe a tree trunk and branches on top of cake.

5. For decorative leaves, divide the reserved frosting between 2 small bowls. Add red food coloring to 1 bowl; stir to combine. Add yellow food coloring to other bowl; stir to combine. Cut a small hole in the tip of a pastry bag; insert #21 star tip. Spoon the frostings alternately into the bag. Pipe frosting on top of cake to resemble leaves of tree.

1 PIECE: 475 cal., 11g fat (5g sat. fat), 54mg chol., 205mg sod., 90g carb. (72g sugars, 1g fiber), 6g pro.

KITCHEN TIP: If you're new to piping frosting on a cake, do a test run on a sheet of parchment or waxed paper to get used to how the frosting flows out of the piping bag.

WINTER GATHERINGS

Holiday
Open House

Potluck Sausage Casserole

Brie Appetizers with
Bacon-Plum Jam

Festive Holiday Punch

Cocktail Mushroom Meatballs

Holiday Chicken &
Sausage Wreath

Brandied Blue
Cheese Spread

Lemon Snowball

POTLUCK SAUSAGE CASSEROLE

Whenever my husband digs in to this pasta casserole, full of Italian sausage and veggies, he gets a big smile on his face. I love that!

—Jane Davis, Marion, IN

PREP: 25 MIN. • **BAKE:** 25 MIN. + STANDING • **MAKES:** 10 SERVINGS

1 pkg. (16 oz.) penne pasta
1 lb. bulk Italian sausage
1 Tbsp. butter
1 Tbsp. olive oil
1 medium onion, finely chopped
1 medium carrot, finely chopped
1½ tsp. dried oregano
1 tsp. salt
½ tsp. pepper
1 small zucchini, halved lengthwise and sliced
1 cup chopped fresh mushrooms
6 garlic cloves, minced
1 can (15 oz.) tomato sauce
1 jar (14 oz.) pasta sauce with meat
2 cups shredded part-skim mozzarella cheese
  Minced fresh parsley, optional

1. Preheat oven to 350°. Cook pasta according to package directions for al dente; drain and transfer to greased 13x9-in. baking dish. Meanwhile, in a large skillet, cook sausage over medium heat until no longer pink, 6-8 minutes, breaking into crumbles; drain and remove from pan.

2. In same skillet, heat butter and oil over medium-high heat. Add onion, carrot, oregano, salt and pepper; cook and stir 5 minutes. Add zucchini, mushrooms and garlic; cook and stir 6-8 minutes longer or until vegetables are tender.

3. Stir in tomato sauce, pasta sauce and sausage; pour over pasta. Sprinkle with cheese (dish will be full). Cover casserole with a piece of foil coated with cooking spray. Bake 10 minutes. Uncover; bake 15-20 minutes longer or until golden brown and cheese is melted. If desired, sprinkle with fresh parsley. Let stand 10 minutes before serving.

1⅓ CUPS: 408 cal., 19g fat (7g sat. fat), 42mg chol., 1104mg sod., 44g carb. (7g sugars, 4g fiber), 18g pro.

KITCHEN TIP: Save time by assembling this dish the day before the party. Simply cover the casserole and store it in the fridge overnight. Set the entree out 30 minutes before baking, and bake as directed.

BRIE APPETIZERS WITH BACON-PLUM JAM

Among my friends, I'm known as the Pork Master because I love to cook
just about every cut there is. These appetizers combine soft, mild Brie cheese
with a sweet-sour bacon jam that has a touch of Sriracha sauce.

—*Rick Pascocello, New York, NY*

PREP: 25 MIN. • COOK: 1¼ HOURS • MAKES: 2½ DOZEN

1 lb. bacon strips, chopped
1 cup thinly sliced
   sweet onion
1 shallot, finely chopped
5 garlic cloves, minced
1 cup brewed coffee
½ cup water
¼ cup cider vinegar
¼ cup pitted dried
   plums (prunes),
   coarsely chopped
3 Tbsp. brown sugar
1 Tbsp. maple syrup
1 Tbsp. Sriracha chili sauce
½ tsp. pepper
30 slices Brie cheese
   (¼ in. thick)
30 slices French bread
   baguette (¼ in.
   thick), toasted

1. In a large skillet, cook bacon over medium heat until partially cooked but not crisp. Remove to paper towels with a slotted spoon; drain skillet, reserving 1 Tbsp. drippings.

2. Add onion and shallot to drippings; cook and stir 5 minutes. Add garlic; cook 2 minutes longer. Stir in coffee, water, vinegar, plums, brown sugar, maple syrup, chili sauce and pepper. Bring to a boil. Stir in bacon. Reduce heat; simmer, uncovered, until liquid is syrupy, stirring occasionally, 1¼-1½ hours. Remove from heat. Cool to room temperature.

3. Transfer mixture to a food processor; pulse until jam reaches desired consistency. Place cheese slices on toasted baguette slices. Top each with 2 tsp. jam.

1 APPETIZER: 91 cal., 5g fat (3g sat. fat), 17mg chol., 205mg sod., 6g carb. (3g sugars, 0 fiber), 4g pro.

FESTIVE HOLIDAY PUNCH

This refreshing holiday punch has a gorgeous raspberry color and tangy flavor.
To complete the magic, we garnish the glasses with lime wedges.

—*Tahnia Fox, Trenton, MI*

TAKES: 5 MIN. • **MAKES:** 14 SERVINGS (ABOUT 2¾ QT.)

1 **bottle (64 oz.) cranberry-raspberry juice, chilled**
1 **can (12 oz.) frozen raspberry lemonade concentrate, thawed**
1 **bottle (2 liters) lemon-lime soda, chilled**
Fresh raspberries
Ice cubes
Lime wedges, optional

In a punch bowl, mix juice and lemonade concentrate. Stir in soda; top with raspberries. Serve over ice. If desired, garnish glasses with lime wedges.

¾ CUP: 185 cal., 0 fat (0 sat. fat), 0 chol., 21mg sod., 47g carb. (43g sugars, 0 fiber), 0 pro.

KITCHEN TIP: For a splash of color, add a few lime wedges to the punch bowl along with the raspberries.

LET IT SNOW!

To make a beautiful display for your buffet, the best option might be the thrift store! This display of homemade snow globes was created from a collection of old glass items—cookie jars, glass hurricanes and candlesticks—found in secondhand shops. Vintage ornaments, Christmas decor and toys were selected and arranged to create charming scenes. Cotton batting and bagged snowflakes from the craft store fill the bottom of the containers, and carefully trimmed bottle brushes make the perfect white trees. Let your imagination run wild—if you prefer everything at your party to be edible, create scenes using gingerbread cutouts, with sanding sugar as snow!

COCKTAIL MUSHROOM MEATBALLS

Tide over even the biggest appetites with beef-and-pork meatballs in a chunky mushroom sauce. Larger portions served over noodles or rice make a great dinner, too.

—*Kelley Diane, Madison, WI*

PREP: 40 MIN. • **COOK:** 25 MIN. • **MAKES:** ABOUT 4½ DOZEN

1 large egg
1 envelope onion soup mix
¼ cup dry bread crumbs
1½ tsp. Worcestershire sauce
1½ lbs. ground beef
½ lb. bulk pork sausage

SAUCE
1 Tbsp. olive oil
1 Tbsp. butter
½ lb. sliced baby portobello mushrooms
½ lb. sliced fresh mushrooms
1 small onion, halved and sliced
1 garlic clove, minced
1 envelope brown gravy mix
1 tsp. minced fresh thyme
1 cup water
¼ cup white wine
1 can (10¾ oz.) condensed cream of mushroom soup, undiluted
¼ tsp. coarsely ground pepper

1. Preheat oven to 400°. In a large bowl, whisk egg, soup mix, bread crumbs and Worcestershire sauce. Add beef and pork sausage; mix lightly but thoroughly. Shape into 1-in. balls. Place meatballs on a greased rack in a 15x10x1-in. baking pan. Bake 12-15 minutes or until browned.

2. Meanwhile, in a 6-qt. stockpot, heat oil and butter over medium-high heat. Add mushrooms and onion; cook and stir 6-8 minutes or until tender. Add garlic; cook 1 minute longer. Stir in brown gravy mix and thyme. Add the water and wine; bring to a boil, stirring constantly. Cook and stir 1-2 minutes or until thickened.

3. Stir in condensed soup, pepper and meatballs; return to a boil. Reduce heat; simmer, covered, 15-20 minutes or until meatballs are cooked through.

1 MEATBALL: 48 cal., 3g fat (1g sat. fat), 13mg chol., 142mg sod., 2g carb. (0 sugars, 0 fiber), 3g pro.

HOLIDAY CHICKEN & SAUSAGE WREATH

Hearty enough to cut into larger slices as a main dish, this golden wreath brims with a delicious, ooey-gooey meat filling. You'll want to make this one year-round!

—Jane Whittaker, Pensacola, FL

PREP: 30 MIN. • **BAKE:** 25 MIN. + STANDING • **MAKES:** 16 SERVINGS

2 tubes (8 oz. each) refrigerated crescent rolls
½ lb. bulk pork sausage
1 carton (8 oz.) spreadable chive and onion cream cheese
1 can (8 oz.) sliced water chestnuts, drained and finely chopped
1¼ cups shredded Swiss cheese
1¼ cups shredded part-skim mozzarella cheese
1¼ cups cubed cooked chicken
3 green onions, chopped
2 jalapeno peppers, seeded and minced
¼ cup finely chopped sweet red pepper
¼ cup finely chopped green pepper
3 Tbsp. coleslaw salad dressing
2 tsp. Worcestershire sauce
1 tsp. hot pepper sauce
¼ tsp. pepper

1. Preheat oven to 375°. Unroll crescent dough and separate into triangles. On an ungreased 12-in. pizza pan, arrange triangles in a ring with points toward the outside, wide ends overlapping and leaving a 3-in. circle open in center. Press overlapping edges of dough to seal.

2. In a large skillet, cook sausage over medium heat until no longer pink, 4-6 minutes, breaking into crumbles; drain and transfer to a large bowl. Stir in remaining ingredients.

3. Spoon mixture across wide end of triangles. Fold pointed ends of triangles over filling, tucking points under to form a ring (filling will be visible). Bake 25-30 minutes or until golden brown. Let stand 15 minutes before slicing.

NOTE: Wear disposable gloves when cutting hot peppers; the oils can burn skin. Avoid touching your face.

1 PIECE: 273 cal., 17g fat (8g sat. fat), 41mg chol., 471mg sod., 17g carb. (5g sugars, 1g fiber), 12g pro.

HOW TO ASSEMBLE

STEP 1
Arrange dough triangles in a ring as directed. Set a small bowl in the center to ensure an even opening for a wreath shape. Remove the bowl.

STEP 2
Spoon filling onto the ring. There is a lot of filling so you'll need to gently stretch the pointed triangle ends over it. Be sure to tuck pointed ends underneath the ring so the dough won't bake into the center of the ring.

BRANDIED BLUE CHEESE SPREAD

Pour on the holiday spirit with a splash of brandy and three kinds of cheese.
Pumpkin seeds, or pepitas, are a crunchy topping for the smooth spread.

—*T.B. England, San Antonio, TX*

PREP: 15 MIN. + CHILLING • MAKES: ABOUT 2 CUPS

1   pkg. (8 oz.) cream
    cheese, softened
1   pkg. (4 oz.) garlic-herb
    spreadable cheese
¾   cup crumbled
    blue cheese
2   Tbsp. brandy
1   shallot, finely chopped
1   Tbsp. minced
    fresh parsley
1   Tbsp. honey
⅛   tsp. salt
    Dash pepper
¼   cup salted pumpkin
    seeds or pepitas
    Assorted crackers or
    apple slices

1. In a small bowl, mix the first 9 ingredients until blended. Transfer to a serving dish; sprinkle with pumpkin seeds.

2. Refrigerate, covered, 2 hours before serving. Serve with crackers or apples.

2 TBSP.: 121 cal., 11g fat (6g sat. fat), 27mg chol., 183mg sod., 3g carb. (2g sugars, 0 fiber), 3g pro.

DECOUPAGED SILHOUETTE PLATES

Arrange these holiday home accents on a wall with adhesive plate hangers.

MATERIALS

☐ White plates of various sizes

☐ Scrapbook or other decorative paper

☐ Decoupage glue

☐ Clear matte varnish spray

☐ Cookie cutters or other design templates

☐ Paintbrush

☐ Craft knife or scissors

☐ Cutting mat

STEP 1
Clean and dry plates thoroughly.

STEP 2
Trace cookie cutter shapes or other design templates separately onto the wrong side of desired scrapbook paper. Cut out the paper shapes.

STEP 3
With paintbrush, apply a thin coat of decoupage glue over the entire face of a plate, using even strokes.

STEP 4
Carefully position a paper cutout where desired on the plate.

STEP 5
Using paintbrush, apply a thin coat of decoupage glue over paper cutout to seal. Let dry. Apply another thin coat of decoupage glue over the entire face of the plate, using even strokes.

STEP 6
Add desired paper designs to the remaining plates the same as before. Let dry completely.

STEP 7
Spray the plates with a thin coat of clear varnish. Let plates dry completely before displaying.

NOTE
Decoupaged plates are not food-safe and are for decorative use only.

LEMON SNOWBALL

For a special occasion like a church supper, I make this beautiful dessert.
Lemon and coconut go wonderfully together—and it just looks like Christmas!

—Lucy Rickers, Bonsall, CA

PREP: 25 MIN. + CHILLING • MAKES: 20 SERVINGS

2 envelopes unflavored
   gelatin
¼ cup cold water
1 cup boiling water
1 cup sugar
1 can (12 oz.) frozen orange
   juice concentrate, thawed
2 Tbsp. grated lemon zest
2 Tbsp. lemon juice
   Dash salt
3 cups heavy whipping
   cream, divided
1 prepared angel food
   cake (8 to 10 oz.), cubed
¼ cup confectioners' sugar
½ cup sweetened
   shredded coconut

1. Sprinkle the gelatin over cold water. Let stand 5 minutes. Add boiling water; stir until gelatin is dissolved. Add next 5 ingredients; mix well. Refrigerate, stirring occasionally, until mixture begins to thicken, about 25 minutes.

2. In another bowl, beat 2 cups cream until stiff peaks form; fold into lemon mixture. Line a 12-cup bowl with plastic wrap. Layer with 1 cup each lemon filling and cake cubes. Repeat the layers 5 times; top with remaining filling. Refrigerate, covered, 6 hours or up to 2 days.

3. To serve, invert bowl onto a large serving platter. Remove plastic wrap. Beat confectioners' sugar and remaining cream until stiff peaks form; spread over cake. Sprinkle with coconut.

1 PIECE: 268 cal., 14g fat (9g sat. fat), 49mg chol., 199mg sod., 33g carb. (30g sugars, 1g fiber), 3g pro.

Grandma's Special Menu

Party Cheese Balls

Greens with Hot Bacon Dressing

Grandma's Yeast Rolls

Herbed Rib Roast

Mashed Potatoes with Horseradish

Marmalade Candied Carrots

Cran-Raspberry Gelatin Salad

Zucchini Parmesan

Cherry Cheesecake

Gram's Gingerbread Cake

PARTY CHEESE BALLS

These tangy cheese balls are guaranteed to spread cheer at your next gathering.
The ingredients create a colorful presentation and a savory combination of flavors.

—Shirley Hoerman, Nekoosa, WI

PREP: 20 MIN. + CHILLING • **MAKES:** 2 CHEESE BALLS (1¾ CUPS EACH)

1 pkg. (8 oz.) cream
   cheese, softened
2 cups shredded
   cheddar cheese
1 jar (5 oz.) sharp American
   cheese spread
1 jar (5 oz.) pimiento spread
3 Tbsp. finely
   chopped onion
1 Tbsp. lemon juice
1 tsp. Worcestershire
   sauce
   Dash garlic salt
½ cup minced fresh parsley
½ cup chopped
   pecans, toasted
   Assorted crackers

1. In a large bowl, beat the first 8 ingredients until blended. Cover and refrigerate until easily handled, about 45 minutes.

2. Shape into 2 balls; roll in parsley and pecans. Cover and refrigerate. Remove from the refrigerator 15 minutes before serving with crackers.

2 TBSP.: 99 cal., 9g fat (5g sat. fat), 25mg chol., 188mg sod., 2g carb. (1g sugars, 0 fiber), 4g pro.

KITCHEN TIP: This is a great appetizer to make ahead when time is at a premium. Wrap tightly in plastic wrap and store in the refrigerator 1 or 2 days before the party.

GREENS WITH HOT BACON DRESSING

Growing up in a German community, I ate this salad often. It's an old traditional dish—I recall my grandmother talking about her mother making this recipe. As a variation, the old-timers in my family cut up some boiled potatoes on dinner plates, then serve the warm salad mixture on top.

—Robert Enigk, Canastota, NY

TAKES: 20 MIN. • MAKES: 8 SERVINGS

4 **cups torn fresh spinach**
4 **cups torn iceberg lettuce**
3 **celery ribs, sliced**
½ **cup chopped red onion**
4 **bacon strips, diced**
1 **large egg**
⅔ **cup water**
⅓ **cup cider vinegar**
2 **tsp. sugar**
2 **tsp. cornstarch**
½ **tsp. salt**
¼ **tsp. pepper**

In a salad bowl, toss spinach, lettuce, celery and onion; set aside. In a large skillet, cook bacon until crisp; remove with a slotted spoon to paper towels to drain. Discard all but 2 Tbsp. drippings. In a small bowl, beat egg; add water and mix well. Add to the drippings. Combine vinegar, sugar, cornstarch, salt and pepper; add to skillet. Bring to a boil; stirring constantly. Remove from the heat; pour over salad. Add bacon. Toss and serve immediately.

1 SERVING: 93 cal., 7g fat (3g sat. fat), 34mg chol., 266mg sod., 5g carb. (3g sugars, 1g fiber), 3g pro.

SCENT THE SEASON WITH POTPOURRI

Set the mood for your winter gathering with this homespun aromatic.

INGREDIENTS
☐ 10 whole cloves

☐ 6 whole allspice

☐ 5 whole star anise

☐ 3 slices fresh gingerroot

☐ 3 pieces of orange, lemon or lime peel

☐ 2 cinnamon sticks (3 in.)

STEP 1
Place the cloves, allspice, cardamom, star anise, ginger, orange peel and cinnamon sticks on a double thickness of cheesecloth. Bring up corners of cloth; tie with string to form a bag. Set aside.

STEP 2
Fill Dutch oven or large stockpot two-thirds of the way full with water. Add spice bag. Bring to a boil; reduce the heat and simmer, replenishing water as necessary.

GRANDMA'S YEAST ROLLS

My grandmother used to make these rolls for family get-togethers and holidays.
They look so special, but they actually come together somewhat easily.
—*Nancy Spoth, Festus, MO*

PREP: 20 MIN. + RISING • **BAKE:** 15 MIN. • **MAKES:** 2 DOZEN

1 pkg. (¼ oz.) active
   dry yeast
1 cup 2% milk (110° to 115°)
¼ cup sugar
¼ cup unsweetened
   applesauce
2 large egg whites, room
   temperature, beaten
1 tsp. salt
3½ to 4 cups all-purpose
   flour

1. In a large bowl, dissolve yeast in warm milk. Add the sugar, applesauce, egg whites, salt and 2 cups flour; beat until smooth. Stir in enough remaining flour to form a soft dough.

2. Turn onto a lightly floured surface; knead until smooth and elastic, 6-8 minutes (dough will be slightly sticky). Place in a bowl coated with cooking spray, turning once to coat top. Cover and let rise in a warm place until doubled, about 1 hour.

3. Turn dough onto a lightly floured surface; divide into 24 pieces. Shape each portion into an 8-in. rope; tie into a knot. Place on 2 baking sheets coated with cooking spray.

4. Cover and let rise until doubled, about 30 minutes. Bake at 375° until golden brown, 12-16 minutes. Remove from pans to wire racks to cool.

1 ROLL: 83 cal., 1g fat (1g sat. fat), 1mg chol., 109mg sod., 17g carb. (0 sugars, 1g fiber), 3g pro. **DIABETIC EXCHANGES:** 1 starch.

KITCHEN TIP: The applesauce might be an unexpected ingredient in these yeast rolls, but it adds a delightful layer of flavor.

HERBED RIB ROAST

The aromatic mixture of herbs and garlic turns this tender roast into a real treat. Our children and grandchildren look forward to feasting on it at special winter occasions.

—Carol Jackson, South Berwick, ME

PREP: 10 MIN. • **BAKE:** 2 HOURS + STANDING • **MAKES:** 10 SERVINGS

1 **beef ribeye roast (4 to 5 lbs.)**
2 **to 3 garlic cloves, thinly sliced**
1 **tsp. salt**
½ **tsp. pepper**
½ **tsp. dried basil**
½ **tsp. dried parsley flakes**
½ **tsp. dried marjoram**

Cut 15-20 slits in the roast; insert garlic. Tie the roast at 1½-in. to 2-in. intervals with kitchen string. Combine salt, pepper, basil, parsley and marjoram; rub over roast. Place fat side up on a rack in a roasting pan. Bake, uncovered, at 325° for 2-2½ hours or until meat reaches the desired doneness (for medium-rare, a thermometer should read 135°; medium, 140°; medium-well, 145°). Let stand 15 minutes before slicing.

4 OZ. COOKED BEEF: 397 cal., 29g fat (12g sat. fat), 107mg chol., 319mg sod., 0 carb. (0 sugars, 0 fiber), 32g pro.

FRESH HERBS AS DECOR

For a festive and aromatic touch, tuck fresh herbs through the napkin ring at each place setting. You can go with a single type of herb for the whole table, or give different herbs to the guests—may we recommend parsley, sage, rosemary and thyme? Don't overdo it, or your place setting will look as if it contains a bouquet garnish, but a single sprig is a lovely touch.

MASHED POTATOES WITH HORSERADISH

Unlike ordinary garlic mashed potatoes, this unusual but delicious recipe calls for prepared horseradish. This side dish, which my family requests when the temperature dips, is also fantastic with roast beef.
—*Cynthia Gobeli, Norton, OH*

TAKES: 25 MIN. • MAKES: 8 SERVINGS

6   **medium potatoes, peeled and cubed**
¼   **cup butter, melted**
¾   **tsp. salt**
⅛   **tsp. pepper**
½   **cup sour cream**
2   **Tbsp. prepared horseradish**

Place potatoes in a large saucepan and cover with water. Bring to a boil. Reduce heat and cook for 10 minutes or until tender; drain. Add butter, salt and pepper. Mash potatoes. Beat in the sour cream and horseradish.

1 CUP: 175 cal., 8g fat (5g sat. fat), 25mg chol., 301mg sod., 23g carb. (2g sugars, 2g fiber), 3g pro.

MARMALADE CANDIED CARROTS

My crisp-tender carrots have a citrusy sweet flavor that's perfect for special occasions. This is my favorite carrot recipe.
—*Heather Clemmons, Supply, NC*

TAKES: 30 MIN. • MAKES: 8 SERVINGS

2   **lbs. fresh baby carrots**
⅔   **cup orange marmalade**
3   **Tbsp. brown sugar**
2   **Tbsp. butter**
½   **cup chopped pecans, toasted**
1   **tsp. rum extract**

1. In a large saucepan, place steamer basket over 1 in. water. Place carrots in basket. Bring water to a boil. Reduce heat to maintain a low boil; steam, covered, 12-15 minutes or until carrots are crisp-tender.

2. Meanwhile, in a small saucepan, combine the marmalade, brown sugar and butter; cook and stir over medium heat until mixture is thickened and reduced to about ½ cup. Stir in the pecans and extract.

3. Place carrots in a large bowl. Add marmalade mixture and toss gently to coat.

1 SERVING: 211 cal., 8g fat (2g sat. fat), 8mg chol., 115mg sod., 35g carb. (27g sugars, 4g fiber), 2g pro.

CRAN-RASPBERRY GELATIN SALAD

Just like Mom's, this pretty gelatin salad has full berry flavor
without being too tart. It's perfect for any winter dinner.

—Rosemary Burch, Phoenix, AZ

PREP: 15 MIN. + CHILLING • MAKES: 10 SERVINGS

2 pkg. (3 oz. each)
   raspberry gelatin
1 cup boiling water
1 can (14 oz.) whole-berry
   cranberry sauce
1 can (8 oz.) crushed
   pineapple, undrained
1 cup orange juice
   Sugared cranberries,
   optional

1. In a large bowl, dissolve gelatin in boiling water. Stir in the cranberry sauce, pineapple and orange juice. Pour into a 6-cup ring mold coated with cooking spray.

2. Cover and refrigerate until set, about 4 hours. Unmold onto a serving platter. If desired, garnish with sugared cranberries.

1 SERVING: 155 cal., 0 fat (0 sat. fat), 0 chol., 49mg sod., 39g carb. (32g sugars, 1g fiber), 2g pro.

CHERRY CHEESECAKE

When I worked full time and needed a quick dessert to take to a potluck or a friend's home, this pie was always the answer. You can substitute a graham cracker crust or use another type of fruit pie filling for a change of pace. Even the chilling time is flexible if you're in a big hurry.

—Mary Smith, Bradenton, FL

PREP: 15 MIN. + CHILLING • MAKES: 8 SERVINGS

11 oz. cream cheese,
   softened
1 cup confectioners' sugar
1 carton (8 oz.) frozen
   whipped topping, thawed
1 shortbread crust
   (9 in.) or graham
   cracker crust (9 in.)
1 can (21 oz.) cherry
   pie filling

In a bowl, beat the cream cheese and sugar until smooth. Fold in the whipped topping; spoon into crust. Top with pie filling. Refrigerate until serving.

1 PIECE: 464 cal., 24g fat (14g sat. fat), 43mg chol., 250mg sod., 57g carb. (46g sugars, 1g fiber), 4g pro.

GRAM'S GINGERBREAD CAKE

My grandmother first made this more than 100 years ago. As a child, I remember the kitchen smelled like heaven when Grandmother baked her gingerbread. The only thing better was when she took it out of the oven and served it with a generous topping of fresh whipped cream.

—Ellouise Halstead, Union Grove, WI

PREP: 15 MIN. • BAKE: 20 MIN. • MAKES: 9 SERVINGS

1   large egg, room
    temperature, beaten
½   cup sugar
½   cup molasses
5   Tbsp. butter, melted
⅔   cup cold water
1½ cups all-purpose flour
1   tsp. baking soda
1   tsp. ground ginger
½   tsp. salt
    Whipped cream

Combine egg, sugar, molasses, butter and water; mix well. In a large bowl, stir together flour, baking soda, ginger and salt; add molasses mixture. Beat until well mixed. Pour into a greased 8-in. square baking pan. Bake at 350° until the cake tests done, 20-25 minutes. Cut into squares; serve warm with whipped cream.

1 PIECE: 232 cal., 7g fat (4g sat. fat), 41mg chol., 350mg sod., 40g carb. (22g sugars, 1g fiber), 3g pro.

ZUCCHINI PARMESAN

You'll knock their socks off with this easy-to-prep side that's absolutely delicious. My favorite time to make it is when the veggies are fresh out of the garden.

—Sandi Guettler, Bay City, MI

TAKES: 25 MIN. • MAKES: 6 SERVINGS

4   medium zucchini, cut
    into ¼-in. slices
1   Tbsp. olive oil
½   to 1 tsp. minced garlic
1   can (14½ oz.) Italian diced
    tomatoes, undrained
1   tsp. seasoned salt
¼   tsp. pepper
¼   cup grated Parmesan
    cheese

1. In a large skillet, saute zucchini in oil until crisp-tender. Add garlic; cook 1 minute longer.

2. Stir in the tomatoes, seasoned salt and pepper. Simmer, uncovered, until liquid is evaporated, 9-10 minutes. Sprinkle with Parmesan cheese. Serve with a slotted spoon.

½ CUP: 81 cal., 3g fat (1g sat. fat), 3mg chol., 581mg sod., 10g carb. (6g sugars, 2g fiber), 3g pro. **DIABETIC EXCHANGES:** 2 vegetable, ½ fat.

Cookie & Candy
Exchange

Thanks for coming!

EASY TRUFFLES

You may be tempted to save this recipe for a special occasion since these smooth, creamy chocolates are divine. But with just a few ingredients, they're easy to make anytime.

—Taste of Home *Test Kitchen*

PREP: 25 MIN. + CHILLING • **COOK:** 5 MIN. • **MAKES:** ABOUT 6 DOZEN

3 **cups semisweet chocolate chips**
1 **can (14 oz.) sweetened condensed milk**
1 **Tbsp. vanilla extract**
 Toasted finely chopped nuts or assorted jimmies

1. Place chocolate chips and milk in a microwave-safe bowl; microwave on high for 3 minutes, stirring halfway through. Stir in vanilla. Refrigerate, covered, until firm enough to shape, about 3 hours.

2. Shape into 1-in. balls; roll in nuts or jimmies. Place in a 15x10x1-in. pan; refrigerate until firm, about 1 hour.

1 TRUFFLE: 52 cal., 3g fat (2g sat. fat), 2mg chol., 8mg sod., 7g carb. (7g sugars, 0 fiber), 1g pro.

CUTE & EASY PACKAGING IDEAS

Homemade edible gifts deserve creative packages that strike a festive note.

1. SECRET SANTA

☐ 8x5-in. pan with lid

☐ Scrapbook paper

☐ Gold yarn

☐ Pompom ball

☐ Santa gift tag

2. COUNTRY CHRISTMAS

☐ Berry basket with lid

☐ Color twist wool

☐ Beige washi tape

3. REINDEER GAMES

☐ ¾-liter mold jar

☐ Elastic ribbon

☐ Reindeer gift tag

☐ Chalkboard label

4. COMFORT & JOY

☐ 7-in. holiday loaf pan

☐ Cellophane gift bag

☐ Red and white ribbon

☐ Gift tag

CRANBERRY PECAN COOKIES

Each delightful little cookie is loaded with cranberries, nuts and a sweet hint of vanilla. But these little gems start with ready-made cookie dough! Let that be your little secret.

—Louise Hawkins, Lubbock, TX

PREP: 10 MIN. • **BAKE:** 10 MIN./BATCH • **MAKES:** 3½ DOZEN

1 tube (16½ aoz.) refrigerated sugar cookie dough, softened
1 cup chopped pecans
⅔ cup white baking chips
⅔ cup dried cranberries
1 tsp. vanilla extract

1. Preheat oven to 350°. In a large bowl, combine cookie dough, pecans, chips, cranberries and vanilla. Drop by tablespoonfuls 2 in. apart onto ungreased baking sheets.

2. Bake until lightly browned, 10-12 minutes. Cool 2 minutes before removing cookies from pans to wire racks. Store in an airtight container.

1 COOKIE: 87 cal., 5g fat (1g sat. fat), 4mg chol., 50mg sod., 10g carb. (5g sugars, 0 fiber), 1g pro.

MINI BROWNIE TREATS

I like to take these quick and easy treats to potlucks and family gatherings. They're always well received!

—Pam Kokes, North Loup, NE

PREP: 15 MIN. • **BAKE:** 20 MIN. + COOLING • **MAKES:** 4 DOZEN

1 pkg. fudge brownie mix (13x9-in. pan size)
48 striped or milk chocolate kisses

1. Prepare the brownie mix according to package directions for fudgelike brownies. Fill 48 paper-lined miniature muffin cups two-thirds full.

2. Bake at 350° until a toothpick inserted in the center comes out clean, 18-21 minutes.

3. Immediately top each with a chocolate kiss. Cool treats for 10 minutes before removing from pans to wire racks to cool completely.

1 BROWNIE: 94 cal., 5g fat (1g sat. fat), 9mg chol., 52mg sod., 12g carb. (8g sugars, 0 fiber), 1g pro.

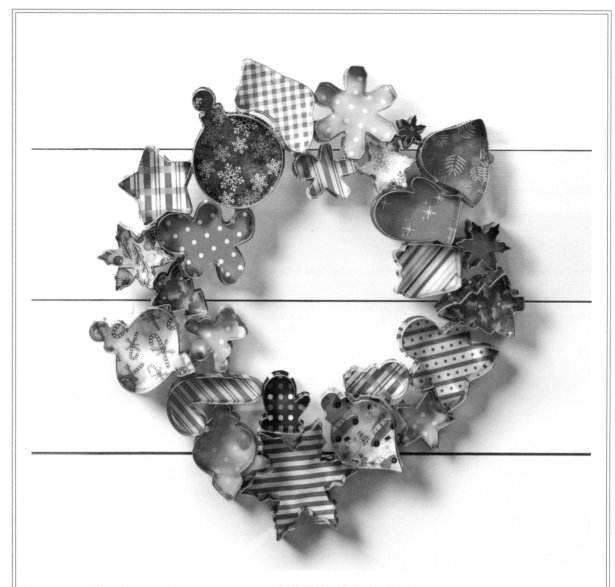

ANYTHING BUT COOKIE-CUTTER

Festive and familiar shapes come together in an eye-catching holiday wreath.

MATERIALS

☐ Cookie cutters, various sizes

☐ Scrapbook paper

☐ Ribbon

☐ Scissors or craft knife

☐ Super glue

☐ Hot glue gun

STEP 1
Arrange cookie cutters in circular form, making sure each cutter touches another at some surface.

STEP 2
Trace cutters onto back of scrapbook paper. Cut out shapes with scissors or knife. Adhere paper to cutters with super glue.

STEP 3
Return cookie cutters to circular formation as arranged in Step 1. Hot-glue cutters together at their touch points.

STEP 4
If desired, hot-glue an empty cookie cutter at top and loop a ribbon through to hang the wreath. Otherwise, just hang the open center of the wreath over a hanger or hook.

SUGAR DOVES

I love spending a cold winter evening decorating these charming little sugar doves. Want to get in the holiday spirit? Start with these doves.

—Peggy Preston, Fenton, IA

PREP: 30 MIN. + CHILLING • **BAKE:** 10 MIN./BATCH + COOLING • **MAKES:** ABOUT 7½ DOZEN

1 cup butter, softened
2 cups sugar
2 large eggs, room temperature
2 Tbsp. 2% milk
2 tsp. vanilla extract
4¼ cups all-purpose flour
2 tsp. baking powder
¼ tsp. salt

FROSTING
½ cup shortening
3¾ cups confectioners' sugar
2 Tbsp. 2% milk
1 tsp. almond extract
½ tsp. vanilla extract
1 to 2 Tbsp. water
4½ cups sliced almonds
3½ cups finely chopped walnuts
Miniature semisweet chocolate chips

1. In a large bowl, cream butter and sugar until light and fluffy, 5-7 minutes. Add the eggs, 1 at a time, beating well after each addition. Beat in the milk and vanilla.

2. In another bowl, whisk the flour, baking powder and salt; gradually beat into creamed mixture. Refrigerate, covered, 2 hours or until easy to handle.

3. Preheat oven to 350°. On a lightly floured surface, roll out dough to ⅛-in. thickness. Cut with a floured 3-in. bird-shaped cookie cutter. Place 1 in. apart on greased baking sheets. Bake 7-9 minutes or until set. Remove from pans to wire racks to cool completely.

4. For frosting, in a small bowl, combine shortening, confectioners' sugar, milk, extracts and enough water to achieve spreading consistency.

5. Frost cookies. Arrange walnuts over the bodies and almonds for feathers. Add chocolate chip eyes.

1 COOKIE: 145 cal., 8g fat (2g sat. fat), 10mg chol., 32mg sod., 15g carb. (9g sugars, 1g fiber), 3g pro.

GINGERBREAD MEN COOKIES

No holiday cookie platter would be complete without gingerbread men! This is a tried-and-true recipe I'm happy to share.

—Mitzi Sentiff, Annapolis, MD

PREP: 40 MIN. + CHILLING • **BAKE:** 10 MIN./BATCH + COOLING • **MAKES:** ABOUT 2 DOZEN

½ cup butter, softened
¾ cup packed dark brown sugar
⅓ cup molasses
1 large egg, room temperature
2 Tbsp. water
2⅔ cups all-purpose flour
1 tsp. baking soda
½ tsp. salt
2 tsp. ground ginger
½ tsp. ground cinnamon
½ tsp. ground nutmeg
½ tsp. ground allspice
Frosting of choice

1. Cream butter and brown sugar until light and fluffy, 5-7 minutes. Beat in molasses, egg and water. In another bowl, whisk together the remaining ingredients minus frosting; gradually beat into creamed mixture. Divide dough in half. Shape each into a disk; cover. Refrigerate until easy to handle, about 30 minutes.

2. Preheat oven to 350°. On a lightly floured surface, roll each portion of dough to ⅛-in. thickness. Cut with a floured 4-in. gingerbread man cookie cutter. Place 2 in. apart on greased baking sheets.

3. Bake until edges are firm, 8-10 minutes. Remove to wire racks to cool completely. Frost as desired.

1 COOKIE: 118 cal., 4g fat (2g sat. fat), 17mg chol., 128mg sod., 19g carb. (9g sugars, 0 fiber), 2g pro.

PEANUT BUTTER COOKIE CUPS

I'm a busy schoolteacher and pastor's wife. I wouldn't dare show my face at a church dinner or bake sale without these tempting peanut butter treats. They're quick, easy to make and always a hit.
—*Kristi Tackett, Banner, KY*

PREP: 35 MIN. • BAKE: 15 MIN. + COOLING • MAKES: 3 DOZEN

1 pkg. (17½ oz.) peanut butter cookie mix
36 miniature peanut butter cups, unwrapped

1. Preheat oven to 350°. Prepare cookie mix according to package directions. Roll dough into thirty-six 1-in. balls. Place in greased miniature muffin cups. Press the dough evenly onto bottom and up sides of each cup.

2. Bake 11-13 minutes or until set. Immediately place a peanut butter cup in each cup; press down gently. Cool 10 minutes; carefully remove from pans.

1 COOKIE CUP: 119 cal., 7g fat (2g sat. fat), 6mg chol., 89mg sod., 13g carb. (3g sugars, 1g fiber), 2g pro.

CHOCOLATE CARAMEL WAFERS

To keep my holiday cooking quick, I've come to rely on fast recipes like this one. The crunchy-chewy tidbits are our youngster's favorite.
—*Susan Laubach, Vida, MT*

PREP: 15 MIN. • BAKE: 5 MIN./BATCH • MAKES: 7 DOZEN

1 pkg. (14 oz.) caramels
¼ cup evaporated milk
1 pkg. (12 oz.) vanilla wafers
8 plain milk chocolate candy bars (1.55 oz. each), broken into squares
Chopped pecans, optional

1. Place the caramels and milk in a microwave-safe bowl; microwave, uncovered, on high for 2 minutes or until melted. Stir until smooth. Spread over the vanilla wafers; place on ungreased baking sheets.

2. Top each with a chocolate square. Place in a 225° oven for 1-2 minutes or until chocolate is melted. Spread with an icing knife. Sprinkle with pecans if desired.

1 COOKIE: 60 cal., 2g fat (1g sat. fat), 2mg chol., 31mg sod., 9g carb. (7g sugars, 0 fiber), 1g pro.

ALMOND RASPBERRY STARS

The first Christmas that I baked these, I ended up quickly making
a second batch! The whole family enjoyed them.

—*Darlene Weaver, Lebanon, PA*

PREP: 35 MIN. + CHILLING • **BAKE:** 15 MIN./BATCH + COOLING • **MAKES:** ABOUT 1½ DOZEN

¾ cup butter, softened
½ cup confectioners' sugar
1 tsp. vanilla extract
½ tsp. almond extract
1¾ cups plus 2 Tbsp.
    all-purpose flour
1 Tbsp. finely chopped
    almonds
1 Tbsp. sugar
½ tsp. ground cinnamon
1 large egg white, beaten
⅓ cup raspberry jam

1. Cream butter and confectioners' sugar until light and fluffy, 5-7 minutes. Beat in extracts. Gradually beat flour into creamed mixture. Shape into a ball; refrigerate, covered, for 15 minutes.

2. Preheat oven to 350°. On a lightly floured surface, roll dough to ¼-in. thickness. With floured cookie cutters, cut dough into equal numbers of 2½-in. and 1½-in. stars. Combine almonds, sugar and cinnamon. Brush the small stars with egg white; immediately sprinkle with almond mixture. Leave the large stars plain.

3. Place all stars 1 in. apart on ungreased baking sheets, using separate sheets for the small and the large stars. Bake just until tips begin to brown, about 10 minutes for small stars and 12 minutes for large. Cool completely on wire racks.

4. To assemble, spread enough jam over large stars to cover centers. Top with small stars; press lightly (jam should show around edge of small stars). Let jam set before storing cookies in an airtight container.

1 SANDWICH COOKIE: 150 cal., 8g fat (5g sat. fat), 20mg chol., 64mg sod., 18g carb. (8g sugars, 0 fiber), 2g pro.

GINGER & MAPLE MACADAMIA NUT COOKIES

This spiced cookie has a real kick of ginger that reminds me of the traditional German lebkuchen. Add colored sprinkles for extra sparkle.
—*Thomas Faglon, Somerset, NJ*

PREP: 45 MIN. + CHILLING • **BAKE:** 10 MIN./BATCH + COOLING • **MAKES:** ABOUT 7 DOZEN

1½ **cups butter, softened**
½ **cup sugar**
¾ **cup maple syrup**
4 **cups all-purpose flour**
3 **tsp. ground ginger**
3 **tsp. ground cinnamon**
1 **tsp. ground allspice**
½ **tsp. ground cloves**
1½ **tsp. salt**
1½ **tsp. baking soda**
1½ **cups finely chopped macadamia nuts**
24 **oz. dark chocolate candy coating, melted**
⅓ **cup finely chopped crystallized ginger**

1. In a large bowl, cream butter and sugar until light and fluffy, 5-7 minutes. Gradually beat in syrup. In another bowl, whisk flour, spices, salt and baking soda; gradually beat into creamed mixture. Stir in nuts.

2. Divide dough in half; shape each into a 12-in.-long roll. Wrap securely; refrigerate 2 hours or until firm.

3. Preheat oven to 350°. Unwrap and cut dough crosswise into ¼-in. slices. Place 1 in. apart on ungreased baking sheets. Bake 8-10 minutes or until set. Cool on pans 2 minutes. Remove to wire racks to cool completely.

4. Dip each cookie halfway into melted candy coating; allow excess to drip off. Place on waxed paper-lined baking sheets; sprinkle with crystallized ginger. Refrigerate until set.

1 COOKIE: 126 cal., 8g fat (4g sat. fat), 9mg chol., 103mg sod., 14g carb. (9g sugars, 1g fiber), 1g pro.

CHOCOLATE REINDEER

My reindeer cookies fly off the plate when my brother is around.
The subtle chocolate flavor beats vanilla cookies, hands down.
—*Lisa Rupple, Keenesburg, CO*

PREP: 30 MIN. + CHILLING • **BAKE:** 10 MIN./BATCH • **MAKES:** ABOUT 3 DOZEN

1 cup butter, softened
1 cup sugar
½ cup packed brown sugar
1 large egg, room
  temperature
1 tsp. vanilla extract
2¼ cups all-purpose flour
½ cup baking cocoa
1 tsp. baking soda
44 Red Hots

OPTIONAL ICING/DECORATION
1½ cups confectioners' sugar
2 to 3 Tbsp. whole milk
  Blue pearl dragees

1. In a bowl, cream butter and sugars until light and fluffy. Beat in the egg and vanilla. In another bowl, whisk flour, cocoa and baking soda; gradually beat into creamed mixture. Refrigerate, covered, at least 2 hours or until easy to handle.

2. Preheat oven to 375°. On a lightly floured surface, roll dough to ⅛-in. thickness. Cut with a 3½-in. reindeer-shaped cookie cutter. Place on greased baking sheets.

3. Bake 8-9 minutes. Quickly press a Red Hot onto each nose. Cool on pans 2 minutes. Remove to wire racks to cool completely.

4. If desired, combine confectioners' sugar and enough milk to reach a piping consistency. Place mixture in a pastry bag fitted with a small round tip; fill with icing. Pipe around the edges of cookies and add a dragee for the eye.

1 COOKIE: 135 cal., 5g fat (3g sat. fat), 19mg chol., 79mg sod., 21g carb. (14g sugars, 0 fiber), 1g pro.

LINZER COOKIES

These cookies have an old-world elegance and a special flavor that delights. The bright red spark of raspberry jam and the wreath shape make them a perfect addition to any holiday cookie platter.

—*Jane Pearcy, Verona, WI*

PREP: 30 MIN. + CHILLING • **BAKE:** 10 MIN./BATCH + COOLING • **MAKES:** 3 DOZEN

1¼ cups butter, softened
1 cup sugar
2 large eggs, room temperature
3 cups all-purpose flour
1 Tbsp. baking cocoa
½ tsp. salt
¼ tsp. ground cinnamon
¼ tsp. ground nutmeg
⅛ tsp. ground cloves
2 cups ground almonds
6 Tbsp. seedless raspberry jam
3 Tbsp. confectioners' sugar

1. In a large bowl, cream butter and sugar until light and fluffy, 5-7 minutes. Add eggs, 1 at a time, beating well after each addition. Combine flour, cocoa, salt and spices; gradually add to creamed mixture and mix well. Stir in almonds. Refrigerate for 1 hour or until easy to handle.

2. Preheat oven to 350°. On a lightly floured surface, roll out dough to ⅛-in. thickness. Cut with a floured 2½-in. round cookie cutter. From the center of half the cookies, cut out a 1½-in. shape.

3. Place on ungreased baking sheets. Bake 10-12 minutes or until edges are golden brown. Remove to wire racks to cool completely.

4. Spread the bottom of each solid cookie with ½ tsp. jam. Sprinkle cutout cookies with confectioners' sugar; carefully place over jam.

1 COOKIE: 161 cal., 9g fat (4g sat. fat), 28mg chol., 82mg sod., 17g carb. (9g sugars, 1g fiber), 3g pro.

KITCHEN TIP: The ruby red color of raspberry jam makes these cookies a standout on holiday platters, but feel free to use whatever jam you like best.

Christmas Eve Appetizers

Golden Santa Bread

Roasted Cheddar Herb Almonds

Tuscan Chicken Tenders
with Pesto Sauce

Avocado Goat Cheese Truffles

Pacific Northwest
Pickled Shrimp

Cranberry-Orange Sangria

Reuben Rounds

Teriyaki Salmon Bundles

GOLDEN SANTA BREAD

A friend of mine shared this fun idea. The finished loaf looks complicated, but it's actually simple to create.

—Vicki Melies, Elkhorn, NE

PREP: 30 MIN. + RISING • BAKE: 25 MIN. • MAKES: 1 LOAF (18 SERVINGS)

4 to 4½ cups bread flour
½ cup sugar
2 pkg. (¼ oz. each) active dry yeast
1½ tsp. salt
½ cup 2% milk
¼ cup water
¼ cup butter, cubed
2 large eggs, room temperature
2 raisins
2 large egg yolks
2 to 3 drops red food coloring

1. In a large bowl, combine 2 cups flour, sugar, yeast and salt. In a small saucepan, heat milk, water and butter to 120°-130°. Add to dry ingredients; beat just until moistened. Beat in eggs until smooth. Stir in enough remaining flour to form a stiff dough.

2. Turn onto a floured surface; knead until smooth and elastic, 6-8 minutes. Place in a greased bowl, turning once to grease top. Cover and let rise in a warm place until doubled, about 1 hour.

3. Preheat oven to 350°. Punch dough down. Turn onto a lightly floured surface; divide into 2 portions, 1 slightly larger.

4. Shape the larger portion into an elongated triangle with rounded corners for Santa's head and hat.

5. Divide the smaller portion in half. Shape and flatten 1 half into a beard. Place beard over face; using a sharp knife, cut deep slits to resemble hair.

6. Use the remaining dough for the mustache, nose, eyebrows, hat pompom and brim. Shape a portion of dough into a mustache; flatten and place on face over beard. Using sharp knife, cut slits to resemble hair. Place a small ball above mustache for nose. With scissors, cut 2 slits for eyes; insert raisins into slits. Form another small portion of dough into eyebrows; flatten and place above eyes. Roll out a narrow piece of dough to create a hat brim; position below hat. Fold tip of hat over and add dough ball for pompom. If desired, using scissors or sharp knife, cut small lines along edges of brim and pompom to resemble fur.

7. In separate small bowls, beat each egg yolk. Add red food coloring to 1 yolk; carefully brush over hat. Brush plain yolk over remaining dough.

8. Cover loosely with foil. Bake 15 minutes. Uncover; bake until golden brown, 10-12 minutes longer. Cool on a wire rack.

1 PIECE: 175 cal., 4g fat (2g sat. fat), 49mg chol., 230mg sod., 29g carb. (6g sugars, 1g fiber), 5g pro.

ROASTED CHEDDAR HERB ALMONDS

I prepared these one Christmas for my son, who was on a low-carb diet. I was afraid he'd be disappointed because he couldn't eat holiday cookies, but these made up for it— he loved them! Save a handful to chop and sprinkle over a green salad or even pasta.

—*Mary Bilyeu, Ann Arbor, MI*

PREP: 10 MIN. • **BAKE:** 20 MIN. + COOLING • **MAKES:** 2 CUPS

1 **large egg yolk**
2 **cups unblanched almonds**
¾ **cup finely shredded sharp cheddar cheese**
1 **tsp. salt-free herb seasoning blend**
¾ **tsp. salt**
½ **tsp. garlic powder**

1. Preheat oven to 325°. In a large bowl, whisk egg yolk; stir in almonds. In a small bowl, toss cheese with seasonings. Add to the almond mixture; toss to combine. Transfer to a greased 15x10x1-in. baking pan.

2. Bake 20-25 minutes or until cheese is golden brown, stirring occasionally. Cool completely.

¼ CUP: 264 cal., 23g fat (4g sat. fat), 34mg chol., 298mg sod., 7g carb. (2g sugars, 4g fiber), 11g pro.

MATERIALS

☐ Varying lengths of ribbon

☐ Large plastic-foam ball

☐ Pine cones*

☐ Thumbtack

☐ Hot glue

PINE CONE KISSING BALL

For a farmhouse take on mistletoe, try these pretty pine pomanders. Hang them inside or outdoors.

STEP 1
Fold a length of ribbon in half for a loop and secure it to the top of a plastic-foam ball with a thumbtack and hot glue. Repeat on bottom of ball, using various lengths of ribbon.

STEP 2
Adhere pine cones over the entire surface of the ball with hot glue.

*NOTE
Make sure to have a variety of pine cone sizes on hand. Attach the bigger ones first, then fill in the gaps with smaller cones.

TUSCAN CHICKEN TENDERS WITH PESTO SAUCE

Golden bites of breaded chicken? You can't go wrong! A green and red pesto sauce for dipping adds a flavorful accent and festive color. Serve the little tenders warm or at room temperature.

—Mary Lou Cook, Welches, OR

PREP: 20 MIN. • BAKE: 25 MIN. • MAKES: 6 SERVINGS

1¼ cups cornflake crumbs
½ cup grated Parmesan cheese, divided
½ tsp. salt
½ cup 2% milk, divided
24 chicken tenderloins
1 cup mayonnaise
¼ cup prepared pesto
½ tsp. garlic powder
⅛ tsp. pepper
1 plum tomato, seeded and chopped
1 Tbsp. minced fresh basil

1. Preheat oven to 350°. In a shallow bowl, mix the cornflake crumbs, ¼ cup cheese and salt. Place ¼ cup milk in a separate shallow bowl. Dip the chicken in milk, then in crumb mixture, patting to help coating adhere. Place on greased racks in 2 foil-lined 15x10x1-in. baking pans. Bake 25-30 minutes or until a thermometer reads 165°.

2. Meanwhile, in a small bowl, mix mayonnaise, pesto, garlic powder, pepper and remaining milk and cheese; top with tomato and basil. Serve with chicken.

4 OZ. COOKED CHICKEN WITH 3 TBSP. SAUCE: 511 cal., 34g fat (6g sat. fat), 76mg chol., 826mg sod., 18g carb. (3g sugars, 0 fiber), 36g pro.

KITCHEN TIP: Cut the chicken into small pieces before dipping in the milk for bite-sized snacks, or leave the tenderloins whole for heartier appetizers.

AVOCADO GOAT CHEESE TRUFFLES

Give guests the VIP treatment with luxurious truffles you can make in your own kitchen. The goat cheese is mild, and red pepper heats up each bite just a bit. Crackers are the perfect accompaniment.

—Roxanne Chan, Albany, CA

PREP: 45 MIN. + CHILLING • **MAKES:** 4 DOZEN

1 pkg. (8 oz.) cream
    cheese, softened
½ cup shredded pepper
    jack cheese
¼ cup fresh goat cheese
1 garlic clove, minced
1 tsp. grated lime zest
1 tsp. olive oil
½ tsp. chili powder
¼ tsp. crushed red
    pepper flakes
1 green onion, minced
1 Tbsp. minced
    fresh cilantro
3 medium ripe
    avocados, peeled
1 Tbsp. lime juice
2 cups salted pumpkin
    seeds or pepitas,
    finely chopped
    Pretzel sticks, optional

1. In a small bowl, beat cheeses, garlic, lime zest, oil, chili powder and pepper flakes until blended. Stir in the onion and cilantro. Refrigerate 1 hour or until firm.

2. With a small melon baller, scoop avocado into balls onto a baking sheet; sprinkle with lime juice. Shape 1½ tsp. cheese mixture around each ball, then roll in pumpkin seeds. Place on a waxed paper-lined baking sheet. Refrigerate until serving. If desired, serve with pretzel sticks.

1 TRUFFLE: 65 cal., 6g fat (2g sat. fat), 7mg chol., 43mg sod., 2g carb. (0 sugars, 1g fiber), 2g pro.

KITCHEN TIP: Overly ripe avocados are not recommended for this recipe. Try it with avocados that are just ripe and somewhat firm.

PACIFIC NORTHWEST PICKLED SHRIMP

This refreshing recipe is one of my husband's favorites. I like to serve the sweet-sour pickled shrimp when we're entertaining. People say it's addictive!

—*Kathy Wright, Highland, CA*

PREP: 40 MIN. • COOK: 5 MIN. + CHILLING • MAKES: 12 SERVINGS

8 cups water
½ cup chopped celery leaves
¼ cup mixed pickling spices
1 Tbsp. salt
2 lbs. uncooked shell-on shrimp (31-40 per lb.)

PICKLING MIXTURE
2 large onions, sliced
8 bay leaves
1½ cups olive oil
¾ cup white wine vinegar
3 Tbsp. capers
2½ tsp. celery seed
1¼ tsp. salt
¼ tsp. hot pepper sauce

1. In a large saucepan, combine water, celery leaves, pickling spices and salt; bring to a boil. Add shrimp. Reduce heat; simmer, uncovered, until shrimp turn pink, 4-6 minutes. Drain; peel and devein shrimp, leaving tails on.

2. Layer shrimp, onions and bay leaves in a 13x9-in. dish. In a small bowl, whisk oil, vinegar, capers, celery seed, salt and pepper sauce; pour over shrimp. Refrigerate, covered, 24 hours.

3. Just before serving, drain the shrimp and onions, reserving ½ cup marinade. Discard remaining marinade and bay leaves. Transfer shrimp and onions to a serving bowl or individual glasses; drizzle with reserved marinade.

½ CUP: 169 cal., 11g fat (2g sat. fat), 92mg chol., 267mg sod., 4g carb. (1g sugars, 1g fiber), 13g pro.

CRANBERRY-ORANGE SANGRIA

Letting this sangria sit in the fridge overnight improves the fruitiness, making it the perfect ready-to-serve drink for a holiday party. It's also nice with a splash of brandy.

—*Maria Regakis, Saugus, MA*

PREP: 15 MIN. + CHILLING • **MAKES:** 10 SERVINGS

1 medium orange, halved and thinly sliced
1 medium apple, quartered and thinly sliced
½ cup fresh or frozen cranberries
1 bottle (32 oz.) cranberry juice
1 bottle (750 ml) zinfandel or other fruity red wine
1 cup simple syrup
½ cup orange liqueur
 Ice cubes

GARNISHES
 Optional: Thinly sliced oranges, thinly sliced apples and fresh cranberries

In a large pitcher, combine the first 7 ingredients; refrigerate overnight. Serve over ice; garnish with oranges, apples and cranberries if desired.

¾ CUP: 263 cal., 0 fat (0 sat. fat), 0 chol., 6mg sod., 47g carb. (44g sugars, 1g fiber), 1g pro.

CANNING LID COASTERS

Transform a few ordinary canning lids and bands into decorative coasters for the Christmas season or all winter long. Your family and friends will find them both fun and functional.

STEP 1
Paint the wide-mouth canning bands and lids with red spray paint. Let dry.

STEP 2
Use a lid to trace a circle onto a cork disk for each coaster. Cut out cork circles.

STEP 3
Stamp each cork circle with permanent ink, centering the stamped design on the circle. Let dry.

STEP 4
Glue each lid to a band. Glue cork with stamped side up to each lid inside band, pressing firmly so cork stays flat. Let dry.

MATERIALS

☐ Wide-mouth canning band and lid for each coaster

☐ Cork disk for each coaster

☐ Red spray paint

☐ Reindeer stamp or seasonal stamp and permanent ink of choice

☐ Super glue

☐ Craft knife

REUBEN ROUNDS

Fans of the classic Reuben sandwich will go crazy for baked pastry spirals of corned beef, Swiss and sauerkraut. They're so easy to make, and bottled Thousand Island dressing makes the perfect dipping sauce.

—*Cheryl Snavely, Hagerstown, MD*

TAKES: 30 MIN. • **MAKES:** 16 APPETIZERS

1 sheet frozen puff pastry, thawed
6 slices Swiss cheese
5 slices deli corned beef
½ cup sauerkraut, rinsed and well drained
1 tsp. caraway seeds
¼ cup Thousand Island salad dressing

1. Preheat oven to 400°. Unfold puff pastry; layer with cheese, corned beef and sauerkraut to within ½ in. of edges. Roll up jelly-roll style. Trim ends and cut crosswise into 16 slices. Place on greased baking sheets, cut side down. Sprinkle with the caraway seeds.

2. Bake until golden brown, 18-20 minutes. Serve with the salad dressing.

1 APPETIZER: 114 cal., 7g fat (2g sat. fat), 8mg chol., 198mg sod., 10g carb. (1g sugars, 1g fiber), 3g pro.

CITRUS WREATH

A picture-perfect homemade wreath welcomes friends and family with the alluring aromas of fresh fruit, spices and herbs.

STEP 1
Trim and snip the assorted greens into 8- to 12-in. lengths. Using covered binding wire, bind together 12-15 small bundles of greenery at 3 points each, leaving wire tails long enough to secure each bundle to wire frame.

STEP 2
Position each bundle of greens on front of wire frame, overlapping slightly; secure wires on back of frame as you go. Trim and tuck in the ends.

STEP 3
Using a toothpick, poke a pattern of holes into 1 side of several pieces of fruit and insert whole cloves.

STEP 4
Attach the citrus as desired using 20-gauge wire pieces. Thread a wire through each orange, lemon and clementine, bending wires gently down at a 90-degree angle on each side.

STEP 5
Attach fruit to wire frame; secure wires on back. Trim and tuck in ends. (Avoid twisting wire too tightly or it will slice through the fruit.)

STEP 6
Make kumquat bundles by threading a 20-gauge wire through 2 kumquats. Gently bend wire ends down and twist together below kumquats. Repeat. Attach kumquat bundles to frame; secure wires. Trim and tuck in ends.

MATERIALS

- ☐ 24-in. round wire wreath frame
- ☐ Covered binding wire
- ☐ Eight to ten 18-in. pieces of 20-gauge wire
- ☐ 7-10 bunches of assorted greens (we used lemon leaf, bay leaf, rosemary, olive leaf and seeded eucalyptus)
- ☐ 10-14 assorted citrus fruits: oranges, lemons, clementines and kumquats
- ☐ Whole cloves
- ☐ Wire cutters
- ☐ Toothpick

TERIYAKI SALMON BUNDLES

If you're bored with the same old appetizers, give this one a try. I serve the little salmon bundles on skewers for easy dipping. Standing the skewers in a small vase filled with table salt creates a festive presentation.

—*Diane Halferty, Corpus Christi, TX*

PREP: 30 MIN. • BAKE: 20 MIN. • MAKES: 32 APPETIZERS (¾ CUP SAUCE)

4 Tbsp. reduced-sodium teriyaki sauce, divided
½ tsp. grated lemon zest
2 Tbsp. lemon juice
1¼ lbs. salmon fillet, cut into 1-in. cubes
1 pkg. (17.3 oz.) frozen puff pastry, thawed
⅔ cup orange marmalade

1. Preheat oven to 400°. In a large bowl, whisk 2 Tbsp. teriyaki sauce, lemon zest and lemon juice. Add salmon; toss to coat. Marinate at room temperature 20 minutes.

2. Drain salmon, discarding marinade. Unfold puff pastry. Cut each sheet lengthwise into ½-in.-wide strips; cut strips crosswise in half. Overlap 2 strips of pastry, forming an "X." Place a salmon cube in the center. Wrap pastry over salmon; pinch ends to seal. Place on a greased baking sheet, seam side down. Repeat. Bake until golden brown, 18-20 minutes.

3. In a small bowl, mix marmalade and remaining teriyaki. Serve with salmon bundles.

1 APPETIZER WITH ABOUT 1 TSP. SAUCE: 120 cal., 6g fat (1g sat. fat), 9mg chol., 93mg sod., 13g carb. (4g sugars, 1g fiber), 4g pro.

KITCHEN TIP: For extra flair, brush the bundles with an egg wash and sprinkle with sesame seeds before putting them in the oven. Garnish the dipping sauce with a sprinkling of sesame seeds immediately before serving.

Traditional Christmas Dinner

Parmesan-Coated Brie

Pretty Duchess Potatoes

Creamy Cremini-Spinach Soup

Candied Bacon Palmiers

Perfect Winter Salad

Flavorful Marinated Pork Loin

Sausage, Kale &
Squash Bread Pudding

Mocha Butter Cream Yule Log

MOCHA BUTTER CREAM YULE LOG

It's become a tradition to prepare this Yule log for holiday gatherings. The filling recipe came from an aunt and the buttercream frosting was my creation.
—*Rosie Flanagan, Buchanan, MI*

PREP: 30 MIN. • BAKE: 15 MIN. + COOLING • MAKES: 12 SERVINGS

5 large eggs, room temperature, separated
⅔ cup sugar
2 Tbsp. all-purpose flour
3 Tbsp. baking cocoa

FILLING
2 Tbsp. plus 1½ tsp. all-purpose flour
½ cup whole milk
½ cup sugar
½ cup butter, softened
½ tsp. vanilla extract
½ cup chopped walnuts, optional

MOCHA BUTTERCREAM FROSTING
1 cup butter, softened
½ cup confectioners' sugar
1 Tbsp. baking cocoa
1 tsp. strong brewed coffee
Confectioners' sugar, optional
Chopped walnuts, optional

1. Preheat oven to 350°. In a large bowl, beat egg yolks at high speed until light and fluffy, 4-6 minutes. Gradually add sugar, beating until mixture is thick and light-colored. Add flour and cocoa, beating on low speed. In another bowl, beat egg whites until soft peaks form; fold into batter. Mix until no streaks of white remain.

2. Grease a 15x10x1-in. baking pan; line with waxed paper, and grease and flour paper. Spread batter evenly in pan. Bake until the cake springs back when touched lightly, 12-15 minutes. Cool 5 minutes. Invert onto a tea towel dusted with cocoa. Gently peel off paper. Roll up cake in the towel jelly-roll style, starting with a short side. Cool completely on a wire rack.

3. For filling, combine flour and milk in a saucepan. Cook over low heat; stirring until thick. Cool. In a bowl, cream sugar, butter and vanilla. Add flour mixture; beat until fluffy. Fold in walnuts if desired. Unroll cake; spread filling over cake to within ½ in. of edges. Roll up again, without the towel; trim ends. Place on a platter, seam side down.

4. For frosting, beat butter until fluffy in a small bowl. Beat in sugar, cocoa and coffee. Spread over cake. Sprinkle with confectioners' sugar and walnuts if desired.

1 PIECE: 351 cal., 26g fat (15g sat. fat), 140mg chol., 217mg sod., 29g carb. (25g sugars, 0 fiber), 4g pro.

KITCHEN TIP: While yule logs are usually reserved for Christmas dessert, the cake rolls make a delightful treat any time of year. Consider adding a few drops of green food coloring to the filling for St. Patrick's Day; red for Valentine's Day; or even pink or yellow for Easter.

PARMESAN-COATED BRIE

This is such a wonderful appetizer! Your guests will be impressed. A golden exterior gives way to warm, melty cheese, making this perfect for sliced French bread or crackers.

—*Karen Grant, Tulare, CA*

TAKES: 10 MIN. • MAKES: 8 SERVINGS

1   **large egg**
1   **Tbsp. water**
½   **cup seasoned bread crumbs**
¼   **cup grated Parmesan cheese**
1   **round (8 oz.) Brie cheese or Brie cheese with herbs**
¼   **cup canola oil**
    Assorted crackers and/ or fresh fruit

1. In a shallow bowl, combine egg and water. In another bowl, combine bread crumbs and Parmesan cheese. Dip the Brie in the egg mixture, turning to coat all sides; coat with crumb mixture. Repeat.

2. In a small skillet, cook Brie in oil over medium heat until golden brown, about 2 minutes on each side. Serve with crackers and/or fresh fruit.

2 TBSP.: 202 cal., 16g fat (6g sat. fat), 57mg chol., 333mg sod., 5g carb. (0 sugars, 0 fiber), 9g pro.

COUNTRY-STYLE TREE GARLAND

Make a garland for your tree with your choice of fabric—a gingham check gives a down-home look, but choose any pattern you like.

STEP 1
Cut 3 strips of fabric 2 yd. long and 5⅞ in. wide. Place 2 strips right sides facing the same way and sew 1 short end together with a ¼-in. seam. Repeat with the third piece to create 1 long strip.

STEP 2
Fold the strip lengthwise on itself with the right sides together and sew a ¼-in. seam along the long edges; leave the short ends open to create a long tube.

STEP 3
Turn tube right side out. Tie 1 end with a short piece of yarn, then fill the tube with table tennis balls—you'll need about 92 balls for a 6-yd. garland. Tie a short piece of yarn between each ball and at the end of the tube.

PRETTY DUCHESS POTATOES

You can't beat these attractive bundles. They offer all the comfort-food flavor you love in packages that are just the right size
—Taste of Home *Test Kitchen*

PREP: 35 MIN. • BAKE: 20 MIN. • MAKES: 6 SERVINGS

2 lbs. russet potatoes, peeled and quartered
3 large egg yolks
3 Tbsp. fat-free milk
2 Tbsp. butter
1 tsp. salt
¼ tsp. pepper
⅛ tsp. ground nutmeg
1 large egg, lightly beaten

1. Place potatoes in a large saucepan and cover with water. Bring to a boil. Reduce heat; cover and simmer 15-20 minutes or until tender. Drain. Over very low heat, stir the potatoes 1-2 minutes or until steam has evaporated. Remove from heat.

2. Preheat oven to 400°. Press potatoes through a potato ricer or strainer into a large bowl. Stir in the egg yolks, milk, butter, salt, pepper and nutmeg.

3. Using a pastry bag or heavy-duty resealable plastic bag and a large star tip, pipe potatoes into 6 mounds on a parchment-lined baking sheet. Brush with beaten egg. Bake 20-25 minutes or until golden brown.

1 SERVING: 158 cal., 7g fat (3g sat. fat), 134mg chol., 437mg sod., 21g carb. (2g sugars, 1g fiber), 4g pro. **DIABETIC EXCHANGES:** 1½ fat, 1 starch.

KITCHEN TIP: Nutmeg adds a bit of down-home flair to these satisfying spuds, but feel free to replace it with some finely chopped chives or fresh parsley.

CREAMY CREMINI-SPINACH SOUP

I love soup any time of year—for lunch, dinner, even as a snack!
You can add cooked cubed chicken to make this a little heartier.

—*Susan Jordan, Denver, CO*

PREP: 15 MIN. • **COOK:** 30 MIN. • **MAKES:** 6 SERVINGS

¼ cup butter, cubed
½ lb. sliced baby portobello
    mushrooms
2 Tbsp. finely
    chopped celery
2 Tbsp. finely
    chopped onion
2 Tbsp. all-purpose flour
2½ cups vegetable stock
1 pkg. (6 oz.) fresh baby
    spinach, chopped
1½ cups half-and-half cream
½ cup sour cream
1½ tsp. salt
¼ tsp. pepper
1 Tbsp. minced
    fresh parsley

1. In a large saucepan, heat butter over medium-high heat. Add mushrooms, celery and onion; cook and stir until tender, 4-6 minutes. Stir in flour until blended; cook and stir until lightly browned, 2-3 minutes. Gradually whisk in stock. Bring to a boil. Reduce heat; simmer, covered, 10 minutes.

2. Add spinach; cook and stir until wilted, 2-4 minutes. Gradually stir in cream, sour cream, salt and pepper; heat through (do not allow to boil). Sprinkle with parsley.

¾ CUP: 219 cal., 18g fat (11g sat. fat), 55mg chol., 952mg sod., 8g carb. (4g sugars, 1g fiber), 5g pro.

BRING THE OUTDOORS INSIDE THIS HOLIDAY

Add a bit of natural flair to your Christmas table by simply wrapping fresh rosemary sprigs around each linen napkin. Carefully insert the cutlery.

CANDIED BACON PALMIERS

You only need three ingredients to make this beautiful and delicious appetizer!
I also like to serve them as a breakfast pastry when I make a brunch buffet.
They are special and just a little different from what's usually served.

—*Jolene Martinelli, Fremont, NH*

PREP: 20 MIN. + CHILLING • **BAKE:** 15 MIN. • **MAKES:** 3 DOZEN

6   bacon strips
1   pkg. (17.30 oz.) frozen
    puff pastry, thawed
¾   cup packed light
    brown sugar

1. In a large skillet, cook bacon over medium heat until crisp.
Remove to paper towels to drain; crumble. Unfold 1 sheet of
puff pastry. Sprinkle with half of the brown sugar and half
of the bacon.

2. Roll up the left and right sides toward the center, jelly-roll
style, until rolls meet in the middle. Repeat with remaining
pastry sheet and ingredients. Refrigerate until firm enough
to slice, about 30 minutes.

3. Preheat oven to 400°. Cut each roll crosswise into ½-in.
slices. Place 2 in. apart on parchment-lined baking sheets. Bake
until golden and crisp, 15-20 minutes. Cool on pans 2 minutes.
Remove to wire racks to cool.

FREEZE OPTION: Cover and freeze unbaked sliced palmiers on
waxed paper-lined baking sheets until firm. Transfer to freezer
containers; close tightly and return to freezer. To use, thaw and
bake palmiers as directed.

1 PALMIER: 91 cal., 4g fat (1g sat. fat), 1mg chol., 70mg sod.,
12g carb. (4g sugars, 1g fiber), 1g pro.

PERFECT WINTER SALAD

This is my most-requested salad recipe. It is delicious as a main dish with grilled chicken breast or as a side salad. I think it's so good, I sometimes eat it at the end of the meal, instead of dessert!

—DeNae Shewmake, Burnsville, MN

TAKES: 20 MIN. • MAKES: 12 SERVINGS

¼ cup reduced-fat
mayonnaise
¼ cup maple syrup
3 Tbsp. white wine vinegar
2 Tbsp. minced shallot
2 tsp. sugar
½ cup canola oil
2 pkg. (5 oz. each) spring
mix salad greens
2 medium tart apples,
thinly sliced
1 cup dried cherries
1 cup pecan halves
¼ cup thinly sliced red onion

1. In a small bowl, mix first 5 ingredients; gradually whisk in oil until blended. Refrigerate, covered, until serving.

2. To serve, place remaining ingredients in a large bowl; toss with dressing.

1 CUP: 235 cal., 18g fat (1g sat. fat), 2mg chol., 47mg sod., 20g carb. (15g sugars, 2g fiber), 2g pro.

FLAVORFUL MARINATED PORK LOIN

Beautifully glazed with a mouthwatering marinade, this
entree is relatively low in fat but still juicy and tender.
—*Paula Young, Tiffin, OH*

PREP: 20 MIN. • **BAKE:** 1 HOUR + STANDING • **MAKES:** 12 SERVINGS

1 cup orange juice
¾ cup apricot preserves
2 Tbsp. plus ¼ cup
  sherry or vegetable
  broth, divided
3 Tbsp. lemon juice
2 Tbsp. olive oil
1 Tbsp. curry powder
1 Tbsp. Worcestershire
  sauce
1 tsp. dried thyme
½ tsp. pepper
1 boneless whole pork
  loin roast (3 lbs.)
1 Tbsp. cornstarch

1. In a small bowl, combine the orange juice, preserves, 2 Tbsp. sherry, lemon juice, oil, curry, Worcestershire sauce, thyme and pepper. Pour ¾ cup marinade into a large dish; add the pork. Turn to coat; cover and refrigerate overnight, turning occasionally. Set aside 1 cup remaining marinade for sauce; cover and refrigerate. Cover and refrigerate the rest of the marinade for basting.

2. Drain pork, discarding marinade; place pork on a rack in a shallow roasting pan. Bake, uncovered, at 350° for 1-1¼ hours or until a thermometer reads 145°, basting occasionally with the reserved marinade. Transfer to a serving platter. Let stand for 10 minutes before slicing.

3. Meanwhile, in a small saucepan, combine cornstarch with the remaining sherry and 1 cup marinade. Bring to a boil; cook and stir for 2 minutes or until thickened. Serve with roast.

3 OZ. COOKED PORK WITH ABOUT 2 TBSP. GRAVY: 229 cal., 8g fat (3g sat. fat), 55mg chol., 51mg sod., 15g carb. (8g sugars, 0 fiber), 22g pro. **DIABETIC EXCHANGES:** 3 lean meat, 1 starch, ½ fat.

SAUSAGE, KALE & SQUASH BREAD PUDDING

Who said bread pudding has to be for dessert? I love to serve this for brunch
or dinner when I want something hearty and a little unusual.

—Lauren McAnelly, Des Moines, IA

PREP: 25 MIN. • COOK: 3 HOURS • MAKES: 12 SERVINGS

1 lb. bulk spicy
  pork sausage
1½ cups chopped sweet
  onion (about 1 medium)
3 garlic cloves, minced
½ cup white wine
1 loaf sourdough bread
  (about 1 lb.), lightly
  toasted and cubed
4 cups chopped fresh kale
3 cups cubed peeled
  butternut squash
1 cup shredded Gruyere
  or Swiss cheese
1 cup chicken broth
4 large eggs
½ cup heavy whipping
  cream
1 Tbsp. minced fresh thyme
1 tsp. salt
½ tsp. coarsely
  ground pepper

1. In a large skillet, cook and crumble sausage over medium heat until no longer pink, 6-8 minutes. Remove with a slotted spoon; drain on paper towels.

2. In same skillet, cook and stir onion over medium-low heat until just softened, 2-3 minutes. Add garlic; cook 1 minute longer. Add wine, stirring to loosen browned bits from pan. Cook until liquid is almost evaporated, 2-4 minutes. Transfer to a large bowl. Add sausage, bread, kale, squash, cheese and broth; toss to combine.

3. In another bowl, whisk eggs, cream, thyme, salt and pepper until blended. Pour over bread mixture; toss to coat. Transfer to a greased 6-qt. slow cooker. Cook, covered, on low 3-4 hours or until squash is tender. Serve warm.

¾ CUP: 330 cal., 17g fat (7g sat. fat), 104mg chol., 831mg sod., 28g carb. (4g sugars, 2g fiber), 14g pro.

KITCHEN TIP: Because it's made in a slow cooker and feeds a crowd, this a perfect contribution to holiday potlucks. When setting the slow cooker in the car, don't forget to pack a serving spoon to save your host some time. Bring along an extension cord as well, just in case you need one to keep the slow cooker warm on the buffet table.

Chocolate Valentine Dessert Buffet

Chocolate Truffles

Chocolate Swirl Delight

Chocolate-Covered Strawberry Cobbler

Slow-Cooker Chocolate Pots de Creme

Valentine Heart Brownies

Cashew Clusters

Chocolate Lover's Pizza

CHOCOLATE TRUFFLES

You may be tempted to save this recipe for a special occasion since these smooth, creamy chocolates are divine. But with just a few ingredients, they're easy to make anytime.

—*Darlene Wiese-Appleby, Creston, OH*

PREP: 20 MIN. + CHILLING • **MAKES:** ABOUT 4 DOZEN

3 cups semisweet chocolate chips
1 can (14 oz.) sweetened condensed milk
1 Tbsp. vanilla extract
Optional coatings: Chocolate sprinkles, Dutch-processed cocoa, espresso powder and cacao nibs

1. In a microwave, melt chocolate chips and milk; stir until smooth. Stir in vanilla. Refrigerate, covered, 2 hours or until firm enough to roll.

2. Shape into 1-in. balls. Roll in coatings as desired.

1 TRUFFLE: 77 cal., 4g fat (2g sat. fat), 3mg chol., 12mg sod., 11g carb. (10g sugars, 1g fiber), 1g pro.

ART WITH HEART

Gather used wine corks (try those from both red and white wines to get this ombre effect) and place them side by side, top side down, in an empty heart-shaped box until the box is filled.

DIY WINE LABELS

Cut scrapbook paper so it's wide enough to cover the existing wine label and long enough to wrap around each bottle. Write the names of the wines on the strips of paper, then wrap around bottles and secure at the back with tape.

PERSONALIZED GLASSES

Thoroughly clean and dry a set of wine glasses, doing your best to keep the free of fingerprints. Use metallic paint pens/markers to write guests' names on the glasses. Dry per the paint pen's directions.

CHOCOLATE SWIRL DELIGHT

I made a few alterations to a great recipe and ended up with an impressive dessert. Everyone loves its light texture and chocolaty flavor.

—*Lynne Bargar, Saegertown, PA*

PREP: 25 MIN. + CHILLING • **MAKES:** 12 SERVINGS

1½ pkg. (13 oz. each)
    Swiss cake rolls
2¾ cups 2% milk
 2 pkg. (3.9 oz. each)
    instant chocolate
    fudge pudding mix
 2 cups whipped topping

1. Cut each cake roll into 6 slices; reserve any broken chocolate coating for topping. Line bottom and sides of a 9-in. springform pan with cake slices, covering completely.

2. Whisk milk and pudding mixes 2 minutes (mixture will be thick); spread onto bottom layer of cake rolls. Cover with whipped topping. Sprinkle with reserved chocolate pieces. Refrigerate, covered, at least 2 hours before serving.

1 PIECE: 331 cal., 12g fat (5g sat. fat), 16mg chol., 382mg sod., 46g carb. (35g sugars, 1g fiber), 4g pro.

KITCHEN TIP: Enjoy this no-bake treat during spring and summer by swapping the Swiss cake rolls with strawberry shortcake rolls and switching the fudge pudding for vanilla. .

CHOCOLATE-COVERED STRAWBERRY COBBLER

This cobbler came about because I love chocolate-covered strawberries. Top it with whipped cream, either plain or with a little chocolate syrup stirred in.

—*Andrea Bolden field editor, Unionville, TN*

PREP: 15 MIN. • **BAKE:** 35 MIN. + STANDING • **MAKES:** 12 SERVINGS

1 cup butter, cubed
1½ cups self-rising flour
2¼ cups sugar, divided
¾ cup 2% milk
1 tsp. vanilla extract
⅓ cup baking cocoa
4 cups fresh strawberries, quartered
2 cups boiling water
Whipped cream and additional strawberries

1. Preheat oven to 350°. Place butter in a 13x9-in. baking pan; heat pan in oven 3-5 minutes or until the butter is melted. Meanwhile, in a large bowl, combine flour, 1¼ cups sugar, milk and vanilla until well blended. In a small bowl, mix cocoa and remaining sugar.

2. Remove baking pan from oven; add batter. Sprinkle with strawberries and cocoa mixture; pour boiling water evenly over top (do not stir). Bake 35-40 minutes or until a toothpick inserted into cake portion comes out clean. Let cake stand at least 10 minutes. Serve warm, with whipped cream and additional strawberries.

1 SERVING: 368 cal., 16g fat (10g sat. fat), 42mg chol., 316mg sod., 55g carb. (41g sugars, 2g fiber), 3g pro.

SLOW-COOKER CHOCOLATE POTS DE CREME

Lunch on the go just got a whole lot sweeter. Tuck jars of rich chocolate custard into lunch bags for a midday treat. These desserts in a jar are fun for picnics, too.

—Nick Iverson, Denver, CO

PREP: 20 MIN. • **COOK:** 4 HOURS + CHILLING • **MAKES:** 8 SERVINGS

2 cups heavy
   whipping cream
8 oz. bittersweet chocolate,
   finely chopped
1 Tbsp. instant
   espresso powder
4 large egg yolks,
   room temperature
¼ cup sugar
¼ tsp. salt
1 Tbsp. vanilla extract
3 cups hot water
   Optional: Whipped cream,
   grated chocolate and
   fresh raspberries

1. Place cream, chocolate and espresso in a microwave-safe bowl; microwave on high until chocolate is melted and cream is hot, about 4 minutes. Whisk to combine.

2. In a large bowl, whisk the egg yolks, sugar and salt until blended but not foamy. Slowly whisk in cream mixture; stir in the vanilla.

3. Ladle egg mixture into eight 4-oz. jars. Center lids on jars and screw on bands until fingertip tight. Add hot water to a 7-qt. slow cooker; place jars in slow cooker. Cook, covered, on low for 4 hours or until set. Remove jars from slow cooker; cool on counter for 30 minutes. Refrigerate until cold, about 2 hours.

4. If desired, top with whipped cream, grated chocolate and raspberries.

1 SERVING: 424 cal., 34g fat (21g sat. fat), 160mg chol., 94mg sod., 13g carb. (11g sugars, 1g fiber), 5g pro.

SOFT-HEARTED HELLO

Extend a warm and fluffy welcome when this wreath graces your front door.

MATERIALS

☐ Yarn (1-2 skeins of each of 3 colors)
☐ Heart-shaped foam wreath form
☐ Card stock
☐ Pink acrylic paint
☐ Pompom maker
☐ Hot glue gun
☐ Paintbrush

STEP 1
Make approximately 70 pompoms using instructions with pompom maker, keeping most 3½ cm in diameter, some 5½ cm, and a few 7 cm.

STEP 2
Hot-glue pompoms to wreath form. Glue smallest pompoms along inner edge to keep heart shape in the middle.

STEP 3
To make the envelope detail, cut a 2x2.-in. card stock rectangle. Draw flaps with a marker. Draw a heart in the center; paint with 2 coats of acrylic paint, drying thoroughly after each coat.

STEP 4
Hot-glue the envelope to the wreath.

VALENTINE HEART BROWNIES

Steal hearts this Valentine's Day with brownies that have cute,
yummy frosting centers. They're simply irresistible.
—Taste of Home *Test Kitchen*

PREP: 30 MIN. • BAKE: 20 MIN. + COOLING • MAKES: 15 SERVINGS

1 pkg. fudge brownie mix
(13x9-in. pan size)
¼ tsp. mint extract
½ cup butter, softened
1½ cups confectioners' sugar
¼ tsp. vanilla extract
Red paste food coloring,
optional
¼ cup baking cocoa

1. Prepare brownie mix according to package directions, adding mint extract to batter. Transfer to a greased 13x9-in. baking pan. Bake at 350° for 20-25 minutes or until a toothpick inserted in the center comes out clean. Cool completely on a wire rack.

2. Meanwhile, in a small bowl, cream the butter, confectioners' sugar, vanilla and, if desired, food coloring until light and fluffy, 5-7 minutes. Transfer to a pastry bag. Set aside.

3. Line a baking sheet with parchment. Dust with cocoa; set aside. Cut brownies into 15 rectangles. Using a 1½-in. heart-shaped cookie cutter, cut out a heart from the center of each brownie. Reserve cutout centers for another use. Place the brownies on prepared baking sheet. Pipe frosting into centers of brownies.

1 BROWNIE: 334 cal., 18g fat (6g sat. fat), 42mg chol., 201mg sod., 41g carb. (30g sugars, 1g fiber), 3g pro.

CASHEW CLUSTERS

I make this recipe for many bake sales at the local community college where I work. They are always the first to sell out.

—*Betsy Grantier, Charlottesville, VA*

PREP: 20 MIN. + STANDING • **COOK:** 5 MIN. • **MAKES:** ABOUT 6 DOZEN

---

1 lb. white candy coating, coarsely chopped

1 cup semisweet chocolate chips

4 oz. German sweet chocolate, chopped

⅓ cup milk chocolate chips

2 cups salted whole cashews (about 9 oz.)

2 cups salted cashew halves and pieces (about 9 oz.)

1. Place first 4 ingredients in a large microwave-safe bowl; microwave, covered, at 50% power until melted, 5-6 minutes, stirring every 30 seconds. Stir in cashews.

2. Drop mixture by tablespoonfuls onto waxed paper-lined pans; let stand until set. Store in an airtight container.

1 PIECE: 95 cal., 6g fat (3g sat. fat), 0 chol., 46mg sod., 8g carb. (7g sugars, 1g fiber), 1g pro.

SWEET STACK

Turn wood slices into mini valentines that can be used to adorn a vase of flowers, hang from a doorknob or spruce up cabinet pulls. Or glue a magnet to the back for an adorable refrigerator magnet that's sure to bring a smile.

You can also create clever name tags for gifts any time of the year. Just change the paint colors.

STEP 1
For each valentine, use a flat brush and regular or outdoor acrylic craft paint to paint a solid purple or fuchsia circle on front of the wood slice to within about ¼ in. of edge. Let dry.

STEP 2
Add coats as needed until paint is bright, letting dry after each coat. Paint a solid heart in center or use a paint pen to write a message.

STEP 3
If you'd like, make a pattern of dots around the design or add other artistic embellishments using the paint pen or the end of a liner brush.

STEP 4
Drill a hole through each wood slice about ½ in. below the top edge. Thread a 14-in. length of jute twine through each hole. Secure the loop with a knot.

CHOCOLATE LOVER'S PIZZA

I created this after my dad said that my graham cracker crust should be topped with dark chocolate and pecans. It's easy to customize by adding your favorite chocolate and toppers. Dad thinks the whole world should know about this pizza!

—*Kathy Rairigh, Milford, IN*

PREP: 10 MIN. • **BAKE:** 10 MIN. + CHILLING • **MAKES:** 16 SERVINGS

2½ cups graham cracker crumbs
⅔ cup butter, melted
½ cup sugar
2 pkg. Dove dark chocolate candies (9½ oz. each)
½ cup chopped pecans

1. Preheat oven to 375°. Combine the cracker crumbs, butter and sugar; press onto a greased 12-in. pizza pan.

2. Bake for 7-9 minutes or until lightly browned. Top with chocolate candies; bake for 2-3 minutes longer or until chocolate is softened.

3. Spread chocolate over crust; sprinkle with nuts. Cool on a wire rack for 15 minutes. Refrigerate for 1-2 hours or until set.

1 PIECE: 349 cal., 23g fat (12g sat. fat), 24mg chol., 133mg sod., 37g carb. (26g sugars, 3g fiber), 3g pro.

KITCHEN TIP: Feel free to top this pizza with chopped peanuts, walnuts, cashews or any nut you like best.

RECIPE INDEX